T0287970

F. SCOTT FITZGERALD AND THE AMERICAN SCENE

F. SCOTT FITZGERALD
AND THE AMERICAN SCENE

RONALD BERMAN

THE UNIVERSITY OF ALABAMA PRESS   TUSCALOOSA

The University of Alabama Press
Tuscaloosa, Alabama 35487-0380
uapress.ua.edu

Hardcover edition published 2017.
Paperback edition published 2019.
eBook edition published 2017.

Typeface: Scala Pro and Market Deco

Cover image: *Tempo of the City*, Berenice Abbott, gelatin silver print, 1938
Cover design: Michele Myatt Quinn

Paperback ISBN: 978-0-8173-5947-8

Chapter 1 is a revised version of an essay that first appeared in the *F. Scott
Fitzgerald Review* 12 (2014). Chapter 4 is a revised version of an essay that first
appeared in the *F. Scott Fitzgerald Review* 14 (2016).

A previous edition of this book has been catalogued by the Library of
Congress as follows:
Library of Congress Cataloging-in-Publication Data
Names: Berman, Ronald, author.
Title: F. Scott Fitzgerald and the American scene / Ronald Berman.
Description: Tuscaloosa : The University of Alabama Press, [2017] |
Includes bibliographical references and index.
Identifiers: LCCN 2017001117 | ISBN 9780817319649 (cloth) | ISBN
9780817391492 (e book)
Subjects: LCSH: Fitzgerald, F. Scott (Francis Scott), 1896–1940—
Criticism and interpretation. | Literature and society—United States—
History—20th century. | National characteristics, American, in literature.
Classification: LCC PS3511.I9 Z557736 2017 | DDC 813/.52—dc23
LC record available at https://lccn.loc.gov/2017001117

For my daughter Katherine

CONTENTS

F. SCOTT FITZGERALD AND THE AMERICAN SCENE

INTRODUCTION

H. L. Mencken and George Jean Nathan decided in 1923 to leave the *Smart Set* for the *American Mercury* in order to show "the whole gaudy, gorgeous American scene" through history, politics, religion, and science.[1] Those disciplines seemed more useful than literature for understanding American society. It was a plausible decision; just a year earlier, the list of Nonfiction Bestsellers had been led by H. G. Wells, *The Outline of History*, followed by Hendrik Willem Van Loon, *The Story of Mankind*. Fitzgerald used these books because he believed that social science was a natural entry into fiction.[2] Also in 1922, W. F. Ogburn had published *Social Change with Respect to Culture and Original Nature*, which made the idea of "cultural lag" part of the national vocabulary. Einstein had received the Nobel Prize, and it was widely understood that the idea of relativity applied to more than physics. Yet diagnosing the world was more difficult—and more intellectually dangerous—than appeared. Malinowski's *Argonauts of the Western Pacific* stated that we were finally ready to know "the origins of human customs, beliefs, and institutions." More important and less likely, "the laws of human behaviour in society, and of the human mind" would be revealed.[3] There were serious doubts from James through Whitehead about the ability of any science to explain the human mind. In that same year, 1922, Wittgenstein ended his most notable work by stating that "even if *all possible* scientific questions be answered, the problems of life still have not been touched at all."[4] Fitzgerald recognized that. He and other novelists knew that they worked within incompatible boundaries.

Social science was influential, and reviewers of novels often used its language of "class" and "group." *This Side of Paradise* (1920) was praised because it accurately showed daily college life, and Max Perkins marketed *The Beautiful and Damned* (1922) as a realistic study of café society. *The Great Gatsby* (1925) was praised by William Benét in the *Saturday Review of Literature* because its characters were "actual" and "memorably individuals of today"; while William Curtis of *Town and Country* added that the book was a "success in a form of social realism" that other novelists had failed to exploit.[5] It has been pointed out in a first-rate study of the reception of *Middletown* that social science in the 1920s was thought to convey reality at least as well as fiction:

> "No one who wishes a full understanding of American life today can afford to neglect this impartial, sincerely scientific effort to place it under the microscopic slide," announced a writer for the *New York World*. The *New Republic* agreed, calling it "a book . . . that will give the reader more insight into the social processes of this country than any other I know." Even the characteristically cynical H. L. Mencken proclaimed, "I commend [it] to all persons who have any genuine interest in the life of the American people. . . . It reveals, in cold-blooded scientific terms, the sort of lives millions of Americans are leading." And the *Nation* declared, "nothing like it has ever before been attempted; no such knowledge of how the average American community works and plays has ever been packed between the covers of one book. . . . Who touches this book touches the heart of America."[6]

Could fiction compete with this *Novum Organum*? Even Edmund Wilson, Fitzgerald's constant advisor (and himself an important reviewer) believed in the new social science. He thought that Hippolyte Taine was the best guide to authorship because his work had shown authors "themselves as characters in a larger drama of cultural and social history."[7] Wilson often mentioned this criterion in letters and essays, which became part of his standard advice to Fitzgerald, John Peale Bishop, and Stanley Dell.[8] Fitzgerald had to work even to set his foundations of observation. And he had to differentiate sharply between social realism and experience.

What was Fitzgerald's American scene? As to time, his daughter, Scottie, insisted that his work covered more than the Jazz Age, identifying his subject as America between the world wars. Even that view should be expanded. Fitzgerald's characters of the 1920s and '30s refer themselves back to the period 1910–20. His essays state why he rejected its ideas—and why those ideas provided him with material for his fiction. As to place, there are reasons for beginning in the provinces. Fitzgerald described the South and the Midwest as they were before the 1920s. We know what Louisville looked like to Jay Gatsby and Jordan Baker, and we intuit its effects on Daisy Fay. There is the big city of Josephine Perry and the suburb of Basil Duke Lee. These are not destinations in themselves but stations on the way to change. Finally, as to relationships: Fitzgerald used the language of social science when describing behavior and ideas. Wilson had from 1919 on urged him to write about social conflicts after the Great War, and Mencken hoped for a satire of the decline of democracy. Both emphasized the study of individuals within real communities so that readers could get a sense of what Wilson called the social "organism."

Characters of Fitzgerald's novels and stories define themselves in terms of known relationships: "Bernice Bobs Her Hair" (1920) explains character as category. It lists "cousins," "intimates," "family," "home-town," "mother," "type," and "marriages." Individuality is determined by community. "The Ice Palace" (1920), built around family and friendship, also emphasizes the permanence of place in the imagination: old houses, streets, and neighborhoods. Most notable is the cemetery, which (like Beaumont Hamel in *Tender Is the Night* [1934]) places the present in history through memory. *The Beautiful and Damned* (1922) covers not only the land of the rich but also working-class and army life in the provinces. In *The Great Gatsby* (1925), Myrtle Wilson and Mrs. McKee think about the infinite gradations of status. For them, style is a kind of social escalator. "The Rich Boy" (1926) begins with the analysis of groups: "family," "clan," and "sets." The Basil and Josephine stories (1928–31) show the tortuous path of individuality through obstacles of family, friendship, and tradition. They are Fitzgerald's most concerted effort to ground his fiction in its milieu.

It was important for Fitzgerald to use ideas his readers understood. It was even more important to ground his fiction on his own experience, putting together his own ideas about social class and relationships. The example of William James was there for anyone who applied ideas to human circumstances—and Fitzgerald knew philosophy. James often wrote that individualism was more important than the artificial containers of class identity restraining it. George Santayana wrote a number of influential essays that coincided with the beginning of Fitzgerald's career, and John Dewey kept the issues alive until after the 1940s. All were centered on the understanding that the social order necessarily changed. Certain Fitzgerald characters resist that idea. When Braddock Washington bargains with God to have today be just as yesterday, he means more than restoring twenty-four hours.

In 1919, *The Economic Consequences of the Peace* by John Maynard Keynes began a new era by explaining why the old one could not prevail. The essay on life before the war first explains why it was seductive: "What an extraordinary episode in the economic progress of man that age was which came to an end in August, 1914! The greater part of the population, it is true, worked hard and lived at a low standard of comfort, yet were, to all appearances, reasonably contented with this lot. But escape was possible, for any man of capacity or character at all exceeding the average, into the middle and upper classes, for whom life offered, at a low cost and with the least trouble, conveniences, comforts, and amenities beyond the compass of the richest and most powerful monarchs of other ages." This was regarded "as normal, certain, and permanent, except in the direction of further improvement." Keynes, however, thought the expectation both economically and psychologically impossible:

> This remarkable system depended for its growth on a double bluff or deception. On the one hand the laboring classes accepted from ignorance or powerlessness, or were compelled, persuaded, or cajoled by custom, convention, authority, and the well-established order of Society into accepting, a situation in which they could call their own very little of the cake that they and Nature and the capitalists were co-operating to produce. And on the other hand the capitalist classes were allowed to call the best part of the cake theirs and were theoretically free to consume it, on the tacit underlying condition that they consumed very little of it in practice. The duty of "saving" became nine-tenths of virtue and the growth of the cake the object of true religion. There grew round the non-consumption of the cake all those instincts of puritanism which in other ages has withdrawn itself from the world and has neglected the arts of production as well as those of enjoyment. And so the cake increased; but to what end was not clearly contemplated.[9]

The war, in Keynes's view, had accelerated the process of disillusion. But it all began before 1914—which is to say within the memory of Fitzgerald's characters of the 1920s and '30s. All of this was accompanied by appeals to "authority" that turned out to be as important as microeconomics. Such appeals were to become Fitzgerald's subject.

Social science often used *class* during the 1920s and '30s, as did Fitzgerald. But he concentrated on another defining term: "generation." He used it to identify the difference between himself and those described by Keynes (and others) as beneficiaries of the past.[10] His blocking characters like Adam Patch in *The Beautiful and Damned* and Braddock Washington in "The Diamond as Big as the Ritz" come from the past to dominate the present through the power of money. But that is far from being the entire issue. Even more important is their generation's intellectual absence from reality: "Now no generation in the history of America has ever been so dull, so worthless, so devoid of ideas as that generation which is now between forty and sixty years old—the men who were young in the nineties. . . . Culturally they are not only below their own fathers who were fed on Huxley, Spencer, Newman, Carlyle, Emerson, Darwin, and Lamb, but they are also below their much-abused sons who read Freud, Remy de Gourmont, Shaw, Bertrand Russell, Nietzsche, and Anatole France . . . they are almost barbarians."[11] Fitzgerald does not mean that the rulers of that generation were without ideas. Its moguls, magnates, "catch-penny capitalists, financial small-fry, petty merchants and money-lenders" used what Keynes sardonically called "true religion" to defend their privilege.[12] That attracted social criticism.

Fitzgerald lived in a milieu defined by resentment of wealth. Much of what he had to say privately and in his work was anticipated by Progressive reformers. In fact, he was anticipated by Theodore Roosevelt, who used metaphors later revived by Fitzgerald. In 1902, Roosevelt attacked the ideology of wealth, describing a tycoon as a "mediaeval castle-owner" who inflicted "the tyranny of a plutocracy" on the public. Roosevelt was particularly concerned with mining, its labor practices, and the startling increase in the value of its assets. One furious critic of mine operators wrote that "the divine right of kings was bad enough, but not so intolerable as the doctrine of the divine right of plutocrats to administer things in general with the presumption that what it pleases them to do is the will of God."[13] The outline was there for the character of Braddock Washington. In 1910, at the beginning of the period that Fitzgerald found especially important, Royce listed some major issues of the era in *The Philosophy of Josiah Royce*. They included public suspicion of "the rights of property" and of "our present family ties."[14] Fitzgerald's characters have dialogues about those two subjects. In 1919, Keynes warned about using cultural "authority" to return to past values. It was, he said, impossible for an international economy to go backward. Fitzgerald describes precisely that when his millionaires use wealth to return to the past. Tom Buchanan in *The Great Gatsby* is captivated by "stale" ideas, and Anson Hunter in "The Rich Boy" has a "reversion" to ideas of the past that allows him to be literally a "judge" of the present. The results for both are catastrophic. Santayana took up the concept of reversion before Fitzgerald wrote his first sentence about the rich being inherently different. He thought the strategy predictable and bound to fail.

Fitzgerald's economic world is more complex than that of Progressivism. Many ideas are poised, then accepted or abandoned: old money is better than new; inherited money is better than earned income; ready money is better than credit; stable investment is better than speculation; expenditure has appropriate limits. Levels of income determine expectations as well as establishing values: Basil Duke Lee finds out how much love is worth when he overhears Ted Fay's conversation; Josephine Perry's father—not quite the richest man in Chicago—understands exactly how to behave at his level. But it would be a mistake to think that Daisy chooses old money over new because it is respectable: Tom Buchanan's pearls do not validate Daisy's character but imply that she has been bartered for them.

Thomas Piketty's *Capital* states that novels have been a reliable source of economic information, and he cites costs and expenditures from Jane Austen and Balzac until the 1920s. Finances in the novel—rents, tenancy, income, investment, and taxation—match those of the actual marketplace. Fitzgerald read Austen, Balzac, and Dickens. Like them, he had a clear sense of prices in our transactional lives. He kept notes on his income. His work covers the costs of every kind of transaction from Basil Duke Lee's tuition to Daisy Fay's pearl necklace. Piketty remarks that in the actual economic world there were three important groups competing for wealth just before the 1920s. By far the smallest was comprised of those with unearned incomes. That group concerned Fitzgerald, but no more so than the managerial class and the "patrimonial" middle class represented by the families of Nick Carraway and Basil Duke Lee.[15] These had to earn enough to maintain a respectable standard of living while putting aside enough for bad times—which is the story of Fitzgerald's own financial life. Like many in the upper middle class, he found himself unable to do both. In Fitzgerald, *neither* income, property, nor investments retain the same value over time. Critics tend to concentrate on his portrayal of affluent expenditure, although Fitzgerald also writes about the inevitable decrease of value that is the equivalent in literature of fortune's wheel. Basil Duke Lee begins his economic education: "His ideas of money were vague and somewhat debonair, but he had noticed that at family dinners the immemorial discussion as to whether the Third Street block would be sold to the railroads had given place to anxious talk of Western Public Utilities. At half-past six his mother telephoned for him to have his dinner, and with growing uneasiness he sat alone at the table. . . . She came in at seven, distraught and miserable, and, dropping down at the table, gave him his first exact information about finance—she and her father and her brother Everett had lost something more than eighty thousand dollars. She was in a panic and she looked wildly around the dining room as if money were slipping away even here, and she wanted to retrench at once."[16] Relative income—the disparity between rich and middle class—is only part of Fitzgerald's depiction of money.

There are different ways of conceptualizing wealth and its public effects. Keynes wrote in 1919 about consumption, savings, and investment. Piketty now writes about inequality between salaried and *rentier* incomes. The recollection of Frederick Lewis Allen, *Only Yesterday*, begins with an event important to Fitzgerald: May Day 1919. Lewis describes how inflation, jobs, taxation, and employment were on the minds of those watching the victory parades. Fitzgerald's story "May Day" is an accurate inventory of daily costs and also an inquiry into the power of "ready money" to shape selves. There is a historical chronology: the prewar Basil stories are about the infinite social arrangements that depend, finally, on income; the wartime Josephine stories examine what we do with the selves that wealth confers; and the postwar works—*The Great Gatsby*, "The Rich Boy," and *Tender is the Night*—show the deep connection between money and uncertain identity.

The Josephine Perry stories may begin with Ginevra King as a model of privilege but quickly open up into a view of a monied society unsure of itself even while it is dominant. These stories are full of interrogations: in one of the best of them, "A Snobbish Story," dialogue is about those public issues cited by Royce. We expect a different kind of discussion at the tennis matches, dinners, and theater rehearsals described by the text. In the most recent study of the turn of century, Jürgen Osterhammel provides one reason for Josephine's preternatural interest in ideas when she already has money, class, and power. From 1910 to 1920, the thinking classes redefined themselves according to interests and activities that defined identity.[17] Status mattered, but being rich, although comforting, was not interesting. Just before the setting of this Josephine story, T. S. Eliot wrote his own notes about the American scene. He thought there were infinite attractions to changing social identity: "all the old ladies with cozy shares of telephone stock, all the clergyman of subsidised goodness . . . and all our millionaires" are role-playing at "a time of lively agitation of political theory." They hoped to be mistaken for unaccountably rich socialists.[18] From Josephine Perry through Tom Buchanan to Baby Warren, Fitzgerald's millionaires want to buy what birth left out: "She knew that she herself was superior in *something* to the girls who criticized her—though she often confused her superiority with the homage it inspired—and she was apathetic to the judgments of the crowd. The distinction that at fifteen she had found in Travis de Coppet's ballroom romantics she discovered now in John Bailey, in spite of his assertiveness and his snobbishness. She wanted to look at life through his glasses; since he found it so absorbing and exciting."[19]

Josephine does look at life through his glasses, or she begins to do that. Fitzgerald has juxtaposed scenes showing the discovery of culture by money. Some describe the genteel blackmail exerted by charities, museums, and theaters over Chicago's monied class. However, Fitzgerald (like Dwight Macdonald and Clement Greenberg after him) understands that those who can afford art want it without mental friction.[20] Money in Fitzgerald wants to see art translated: the ladies of Lake Forest are putting on a vaudeville show featuring Travis de Coppett in a white satin football suit; Josephine dreams of seeing her name in electric lights. The emphasis is not on being an actress but on being adored. The supremely untactful John Boynton Bailey knows that such "bogus society hokum" soothes social anxieties and takes up time that might be spent on troublesome consciousness. Josephine's social visions are accompanied by music, which in Lake Forest is smooth and mellifluous. The blues are whitened. At the tennis match, "there was music on the outdoor platform beside the club, and there was a sound of clinking waiters as the crowd swayed out of the grandstand."[21] The opening phrase, lifted from *The Great Gatsby*, has the same implication of the suspension of ordinary life. On the other side of Chicago at the Little Theatre rehearsal, there is no social assonance. Josephine begins to understand women whose "intolerable inadjustability to their surroundings . . . had plucked them from lonely normal schools, from the frame rows of Midwestern towns and the respectability of shoddy suburbs."[22] The social is itself disintegrative.

The Basil and Josephine stories have been praised for their historical detail. Their social history is first rate, but these stories don't make points from nostalgia. Josephine especially keeps referring to her mind—as does John Boynton Bailey. From the moment they meet they debate big money and the middle class; downstate versus the big city; and, most important of all, the extent to which we accept the suppression of reality. When Josephine makes her decision to stay in the world of money, to leave the world of work and competition, she implies more than a taste for privilege. If there is a central problem in this story it is not moral, not about how good or bad she is. The point of her retreat into wealth is that Fitzgerald is right about human behavior and about those things affecting it.

Josephine (and her age-mate Daisy Fay) have a limited amount of civic freedom and less psychological freedom. In "First Blood," Fitzgerald described "Doctor Jung's theory that innumerable male voices argue in the subconscious of a woman, and even speak through her lips." That looks breezy but involves some heavy lifting. John-Paul Sartre wrote that showing "the intrusion of group thinking in the most secret thoughts of his characters" was one of the great achievements of Dos Passos; Malcolm Cowley thought that it became a basic technique of modernism; Lionel Trilling wrote that there was no possibility of an individual will acting against the internalized coercion of its culture.[23] Both Josephine and Daisy give in to what Trilling called the "seduction" of culture—but not without a formidable agon.

A city commission report of 1915 in Louisville remarks that the city had two kinds of people: those who relied on the past and the new, "forward-thinking people" who did not confuse public with private conscience. The subject was prostitution—which is not an anomaly.[24] Louisville was known for great houses, for great wealth, and for being one of the nation's centers of commercial sex. It was a racetrack city, a city that depended on cash for payrolls, a riverboat city, and the site of American's largest army training camp. The description of Louisville in *The Great Gatsby* is not limited to a static view of houses. Within them are movement, change, and momentary being. Fitzgerald is not so much concerned with a vision of wealth as with the collision of its mores with events. The whole story of Daisy Fay includes a cultural or induced sense of self. Trilling thought the only conceivable thing that might challenge it was eros. That was a difficult challenge for women brought up "in a bygone ladylike way that may be hard for us now to understand."[25]

Fitzgerald wrote about the sources of bygone ladylike ideas. They come from Louisa May Alcott and Annie Fellows Johnston, both satirized in "Bernice Bobs Her Hair," and from Marse Chan and Ruth Draper, who give "The Last of the Belles" its fake antebellum charm. Around 1910, American girls preparing to become American women read material that sent Walter Lippmann into volcanic eruption: "Our literature is written by spinsters for school girls. . . . Instead of taking up the high and difficult task of penetrating human beings . . . it has been content with . . . the accepted sentimentality. The characters of contemporary American fiction are stockworn; they come not from original observation, but from the conventions of writing . . . from a tradition about novels. And they look upon a world incredibly bland and preposterously untrue. They are agitated about problems which never agitate anybody. . . . You cannot send a man to American literature so that he may enrich his experience and deepen his understanding. You can merely pray that when he is confronted with the issues of his life, he will forget completely what he has read."[26] The sentimental novels of Annie Fellows Johnston are of particular interest since they were written about Louisville society and possibly about what Jordan Baker called "our white girlhood . . . passed together there."[27]

The most direct explanation of that line is provided by sentimental novels about the South because little happens to upper-class white women in their pages without the aiding presence of black servants. In the Johnston novels servants are seen working, but their main function (as in the Shirley Temple adaptation of a Johnston novel *The Little Colonel*) is to provide moral support. The second half of the phrase is also important. Jordan, who has few attachments to the past, specifically recalls "girlhood." That implies actual events and experiences in Louisville and also an idea about herself. Fitzgerald and Lippmann understood two things about sentimental novels for women: they were conduct books as well as stories and they followed scripts. A central passage in *The Little Colonel's Knight Comes Riding* describes "juvenile tales" as the origin of ideas about the social self. Such stories are reconfigured for contemporary readers. Johnston's portrait of an author shows her "living in a world of her own creating, more interested in the characters of her fancy than those who sat at table with her." She writes "with a throbbing heart . . . pen in hand" among "the warm spicy scents of pinks and cedars, from the graveyard just outside the open window."[28] All of that is less a failure of imagination than a strategy. The idea of "girlhood" is the main idea in such novels. Freud read some of these (he called them family romances) in 1908 and thought that their aim was to make "a correction of actual life."[29] He noted that there were no real parents in such novels: children led their own lives. Which means that problems were on their scale.

The Josephine stories are not, as Fitzgerald recognized, the equivalent of a free-standing novel. But they are his most prolonged and, I think, most successful attempt to show rebellion against culture and inevitable surrender to it. They certainly should be revalued if only to get an accurate sense of the subjects of dialogue. Daisy sometimes gets lost in Fitzgerald criticism because it is naturally assumed that she represents wealth. In fact, she is a provincial. The burden of her story is not her attraction to money but the eventual domination of her mind by social ideas. Like the heroines of sentimental novels, she is fully equipped to talk about nightingales and flowers and marrying off distant cousins (the last of which is actually an enterprise in Johnston's novels). Her white southern girlhood is certainly real enough—although Louisville was famously the most northern of the cities of the South and entirely conscious of northern industrial values. Daisy is southern because she has been taught to be southern in a way that emphasizes the virtues of childhood. When Fitzgerald looked over the American scene he saw that the most characteristic experience after 1910 was the discovery of how unprepared Americans were for 1920. There is a profound similarity between what happens to Fitzgerald's characters and what happened to the nation.

1

THE IDEA OF SOCIETY

Many of F. Scott Fitzgerald's stories, especially those about Basil Duke Lee and Josephine Perry, retain historical value because of their "remembered details."[1] Yet interpretation of time, place, and our social arrangements was uncertain when they were written (1928–31). Edith Wharton's autobiography (*A Backward Glance*, 1934) begins by stating that the American milieu had only recently become decipherable through the work of European sociologists.[2] In her opinion, the way we lived had never been convincingly explained. That view was widely shared. Edmund Wilson and H. L. Mencken, both mentors of Fitzgerald, often stated that literary descriptions of fact were not enough. Writers needed to know how human relations had been reconceived by social science.

Wharton knew about the effects of Darwinism on social thought and was aware of the role Spencer played. Such social theories were on the grand and Hegelian scale, as were those of Marx, Spengler, and Durkheim who wrote predictive analyses of an entire civilization. However, her statement implies more than a panoramic view of systems. Max Weber's studies of institutions had appeared before the 1930s began. Bronislaw Malinowski and his followers had made social anthropology familiar to a large audience. In fact, one of the great sociological works of the 1920s, *Middletown* (1929), was conspicuously about locality in America; it relied on interviews, surveys, and daily observation of work and leisure. In *Public Opinion* (1922), Walter Lippmann had already stated that "the formal political structure exists in a social environment, where there are innumerable large and small corporations and institutions, voluntary and semi-voluntary associations, national, provincial, urban and neighborhood groupings which often as not make the decision that the political body registers."[3] According to Lippmann, knowing how local social systems worked made us revise and even devalue theories of determinism.[4] The details of daily life needed to be explored, not cycles and gyres of history.

How did theories of social life reach Fitzgerald? Certainly through his own reading and observations, and also through the influence of friends and mentors. Late in life, according to his secretary, Frances Kroll Ring, he recalled that Edmund Wilson had "most strongly influenced his political thinking and reading."[5] Fitzgerald's intellectual education began at Princeton in his freshman year when he met Wilson, who was already editing campus publications, doing his own critical writing—and rethinking American literature. The relationship lasted and, as Wilson noted in "A Weekend at Ellerslie" (1952), Scott "had come to regard himself as somehow accountable to me for his literary career."[6] What divided them was the issue of literature and politics. Wilson wanted Fitzgerald to write about American social problems; Fitzgerald did not believe that fiction was a political instrument. Wilson wanted Fitzgerald to support causes like the defense of Sacco and Vanzetti; Fitzgerald had no interest in activism. He did follow Wilson's advice to describe the American scene in detail. According to Wilson, all writers needed to study specific events and conditions in order to demonstrate local, "organic" knowledge of their subject. In a prospectus for *Axel's Castle* (1929) sent to Max Perkins, he stated that he himself would investigate detailed "social questions" about the war's effect.[7] This was consistent; a decade earlier, in 1919, Wilson had given Fitzgerald a reading list in order to prepare himself for life as a writer in New York. He urged Fitzgerald to copy "realistic" writers like Zola and to produce a war story that was not about the front but instead about military management, the effects of war on civilians, and "the stagnation of the troops behind the lines."[8]

Wilson also—decidedly—recommended theories. He wanted Fitzgerald to drop his *Saturday Evening Post* mentality and his remaining attachment to "the decaying Church of Rome." Wilson thought that Scott's Catholicism (and his own Protestantism) had lost explanatory powers to science and to the secular systems of Marx and Freud. In this case, Fitzgerald agreed, later telling a Saint Paul friend that his own heroes were now secular. In fact, "the Rosseaus [sic], Marxes, Tolstois" did more good for the world than believers in "the silly and cruel old God" of our imaginings.[9] In a 1923 interview, he stated that Freud "has had the widest influence on the younger generation. You cannot begin to conceive how far his theories have spread in America. . . . Why, Freud at third-hand ran over this country like wildfire."[10] In the 1930s, he wrote to his daughter, Scottie, to "read the terrible chapter in *Das Kapital* on The Working Day, and see if you are ever quite the same."[11]

Both Wilson and Fitzgerald knew the big systems. Both knew that social facts did not speak for themselves. There was a key difference: Fitzgerald alluded to Freud, Marx, and others but did not rely on their theories to explain his own work. When he talks about the "world" he describes experienced events and states of mind. Dick Diver in *Tender Is the Night* (1934) describes his "beautiful lovely safe world" before the Great War in terms of "human relations."[12] The great monologue at Beaumont Hamel is about "the exact relation that existed between the classes." Few writers have been more explicit about the components of memory. His characters live in families and endure the institutions of middle-class life. The stories record their education in and out of school. The novels cover books and ideas in more detail, and they trace the development of personal associations. The essays review (and construct) much information about work and marriage. Fitzgerald's description of social relations led the *New York Times* to describe *This Side of Paradise* as a nearly perfect study of "the daily existence" of college men.[13] It was his attitude that caused a different reaction. In his work, leisure is organized around occasions. That necessarily involves the display of privilege. A Fitzgerald story is about a group of individuals connected by—as Edmund Wilson put it in 1922—"exhilarating social activities." Wilson admired such coverage, singling out "Bernice Bobs Her Hair" for its replication of "the organism of St. Paul."[14] Such stories had documentary and also satirical value; he recommended that Fitzgerald do for Summit Avenue what Sinclair Lewis had done for Main Street.

At some point, however, sociology collided with social ideology: Wilson thought that Fitzgerald confined himself to a narrow sector of the middle class, the part with money and without culture. He did not in that same assessment of 1922 believe that Fitzgerald could write a convincing novel about Eastern society because of his disturbing willingness to accept the way things were. In his essay "The Critic Who Does Not Exist," Wilson recommended Hippolyte Taine, Charles Augustin Saint-Beuve, and Leslie Stephen to American writers who needed "ideas" as well as "experience."[15] As the 1920s became the 1930s, he became more political and also more dependent on the language of sociology. He wrote of *The 42nd Parallel* in 1930: "Dos Passos seems the only one of the novelists of this generation who is concerned with the large questions of politics and society; and he has succeeded in this book in bridging the gap, which is wider in America than anywhere else and which constitutes a perpetual problem in American literature and thought, between the special concerns of the intellectual and the general pursuits and ideas of the people."[16] Wilson's essay on George Washington Cable ("Citizen of the Union") became a manifesto for literary knowledge of social politics; in "Dos Passos and the Social Revolution" he reminded critics to "take the social organism seriously."[17] Eventually, Wilson urged writers to do more than know about society and politics. The equanimity he saw in Cable would no longer be enough, nor would the studied political indifference of Scott Fitzgerald.[18] Yet it is worth remembering that Wilson's criticism incorporated the various kinds of social science. He was a Marxist who thought that Strachey should be read against Michelet and that Gertrude Stein is best understood as part of the movement begun by Apollinaire that had "collided with historical events."[19] In short, Wilson wanted accurate details in order to combine them into workable theory.

H. L. Mencken, both mentor and benefactor, found a home in the *Smart Set* for those stories of Fitzgerald such as "The Diamond as Big as the Ritz" (1922) that the *Post* and other mass magazines, in Matthew J. Bruccoli's words, considered "baffling, blasphemous, or objectionably satiric about wealth."[20] But more was involved than editorial kindness. Mencken was an evangelist for literature who gave Fitzgerald a new understanding of writers like Conrad and Dreiser. He developed Fitzgerald's native interest in philosophy, and he knew more about the American scene than any other writer. He was our leading analyst of what came to be known as the American Language. However, Mencken was profoundly biased toward satire and realism—and he disliked modernists, particularly Hemingway. Fitzgerald required more of a subject than the follies of the booboisie.[21] He did not judge the middle class by Mencken's standards but by his own experience. His essays are a mine of information on that life—and one of its great defenses. Even in the early 1920s Fitzgerald became convinced that Mencken's determinism could never explain the complexity of human relationships, and he became deeply hostile to Mencken's valuation of literature as a commentary about democratic life.

Like Wilson, Mencken was devoted to social theory. His book column in the *American Mercury* was filled "with science, sociology, and politics."[22] In fact, the magazine was launched with the claim that it would chiefly cover American ideas and problems as well as the usual "eminentoes" he tarred and feathered. In *My Life as Author and Editor*, Mencken explained why. To begin, he had lost faith in literature by 1920. Current novels were inferior to those of the nineteenth century, while their teaching was in the hands of a priesthood of the written word born to be victimized by fake ideas. Literature, he thought, had failed to describe its great subject—the life of democracy—as well as science. Here is his footnote to history: "I made no attempt, in those days, to formulate a literary theory. . . . No reasonably attentive reader of my monthly discourses, by the beginning of 1917, could be in any doubt about my fundamental ideas, which were, in the main, scientific rather than moral or aesthetic. I was in favor of the true long before I was in favor of either the good or the beautiful."[23]

Mencken turned to the social sciences in order to approximate truth. He understood their faults, belaboring psychology for its failure to develop a unified theory of human behavior. His own solution was "to examine the phenomena of the mind objectively, and with some approach to a scientific method."[24] And for that, the best resource was descriptive science. Mencken praised Malinowski and Hortense Powdermaker for attaining objective descriptions of social behavior. He added that "it is strange and lamentable that so many anthropologists seek their laboratory animals in the far places of the earth. . . . I was in hopes, after 'Middletown' came out, that it would be followed by studies of other American towns." Mencken had set his own example when in Waycross, Georgia, finding "it very interesting to rove about the place and observe the inhabitants at their concerns."[25] That was a less innocent occupation than appeared because Mencken was firmly convinced that American behavior was intentionally disguised by local institutions. The opening pages of *Middletown*, asserting that we must study ourselves "as through the eye of an outsider," must have responded to his suspicions.[26] On that subject, Mencken writes, "I guess without knowing that young blood bubbles in Waycross as elsewhere, and that the local pastors visualize a state of chastity appreciably above that which they actually observe." Sociology, as he saw it, exposed subjects distorted not only by the pulpit but also by business, by newspapers, and certainly by education.

Actual sociology was not entirely a matter of observation. It aimed to be comparative. *Middletown* began with the statement that generational chronology was part of its investigative method: "the year 1890 was selected as the base-line against which to project the culture of today because of greater availability of data from that year onward . . . and the boom begun which was to transform the placid county-seat during the nineties into a manufacturing city. This narrow strip of thirty-five years comprehends for hundreds of American communities the industrial revolution that has descended upon villages and towns, metamorphosing them into a thing of Rotary Clubs, central trade councils, and Chamber of Commerce contests for 'bigger and better' cities . . .

the procedure followed enables us to view the city of today against the background of the city of a generation ago out of which it has grown and by which it is conditioned, to see the present situation as the most recent point in a moving trend."[27] The tactic of measuring the present against "a generation ago" allows *Middletown* to impose a narrative. That narrative is not what we expect. One of the major points of the study is that educational values have not changed in the slightest: "it is almost impossible simply by reading a history examination to tell whether it is of 1890 or 1924 vintage." That statement may be even more important than it looks. *Middletown* cites a specific examination in which two out of three students agreed that "the white race is the best race on earth." The percentage was higher for agreeing that "the United States is unquestionably the best country in the world."[28] The conclusion may or may not be debatable but it matters less than the qualifier. *Middletown* concludes that it is normative—at least in the Midwest—to find individual identity not only grounded in the generational past but also tied to it by a Gordian knot.

What *Middletown* takes for background is much closer to the foreground of Fitzgerald's fiction. It is part of the conscious self and determines decisions in the present. In Fitzgerald, those who think about the past are not old; they do not have a reflective but an experiential consciousness. Even use of the past tense in his prose (think of the plangent repetitions of the word "gone" in "Babylon Revisited" [1931]) conveys something *determinant*. Images from the past and statements about it affect consciousness and character. "The Ice Palace" (1920) reminds us that before our own lives "there was something, there was something! I couldn't ever make you understand, but it was there." In "Dice, Brassknuckles, and Guitar" (1923), the spirit of place demonstrates that "thank God this age is joined on to *something*." In "Babylon Revisited" (1931), Charlie Wales wants "to jump back a whole generation" to make sense of his life.[29] The world of the past had its imperatives—Fitzgerald often calls them "Victorian" to let us know that they have been outmoded, replaced by new intellectual and moral authority. Yet he often tells us how much they are missed. Dick Diver's lost world is more than conceptual; it appears in disguised ways, through images of unvisited graves in "The Ice Palace" and reminders of forgotten liturgies in "The Diamond as Big as the Ritz."

No matter how lyrical, Fitzgerald's narratives take place within the hard lines of a social economy. In his conversation, "Scott paid great attention to the resources of society: social position, the effectiveness and the force of money."[30] And in his stories, status and money govern choice. They are the subject of dialogues, editorial comments by the narrator, and narrative mechanisms that suddenly illuminate the exigencies of jobs, money, and class. In "The Freshest Boy" (1928), Basil Duke Lee overhears Ted Fay's girl reminding him that time is money and that life isn't a musical comedy. He sees Mr. Rooney's dive into downward social mobility. In "Forging Ahead" (1929), he meets Mr. Utsonomia, a Japanese exchange student who happens to be an amateur anthropologist. That will be an important point for Basil and even more so for Fitzgerald. The idea of critical objectivity has been planted in his story not to define Mr. Utsonomia's character—he has none—but in order to state his author's position on writing. Mr. Utsonomia has his own parallel narrative, reversing Basil's plan to pick Yale over the state university:

> "They give me choice back in my country—I choose here."
> "You did?" said Basil, almost indignantly.
> "Sure, more strong here. More peasants come, with strength and odor of ground."
> Basil stared at him. "You like that?" he asked incredulously.
> Utsonomia nodded. "Here I get to know real American peoples."[31]

Does Mr. Utsonomia's decision to trade elites for masses bring moral clarity to "Forging Ahead?" The will to know peasants "with strength and odor of ground" implies that caricature is the right mode for such a choice. Utsunomiya University was in the early 1920s a normal school and aggie college. But the language, wonderfully befuddled, is also familiar. Not only does it echo valedictory sincerities; it also echoes reviewers who resented Fitzgerald's own choice (in Robert Beuka's phrase) to live among and write about flappers and philosophers. Terminology repeats itself: Marya Mannes had written to Fitzgerald in 1925 with an intellectual complacency that enraged him; she wanted him to write about the youthful masses that represented "the fresh, strong river of America." It might, he replied, be even more fresh and strong to reject fake ideas of class virtue.[32] In 1926, Fitzgerald's essay on "How to Waste Material: A Note on My Generation" returned to the novelistic "compulsion to write 'significantly' about America." He thought that the subjects of rural integrity and youth at "the American universities" had become overused in fiction and were by then intellectual jokes.[33]

Mencken recommended anthropology, and Edmund Wilson prescribed sociology, but Fitzgerald understood how difficult it was to translate facts. Mr. Utsonomia appears once more, studying interactions at a party and confusing objectivity with reality: "Mr. Utsonomia was enjoying himself. In the whole six months in America he had never felt so caught up in its inner life before. At first it had been a little hard to make plain to the lady just whose place it was he was taking, but Eddie Parmelee had assured him that such substitutions were an American custom, and he was spending the evening collecting as much data upon American customs as possible."[34] Mr. Utsonomia is concerned with the collection of data because "the concept of culture was substantially an importation from American ethnology (or cultural anthropology, as it came to be more usually known) . . . culture as a concept was introduced to sociologists as they were induced, following World War I, to examine the critical works of American anthropologists (especially Boas and his students)."[35] He is part of a large, visible, and increasingly published movement. But Mr. Utsonomia is going to have some difficulty because of his intellectual limits—and those of the social sciences. No one really knew the effect of ideas like evolution, heredity, and instinct, and it was widely recognized that phenomena were all too easily absorbed into "the fallacy of explanation."[36] Basil is a skeptic but not entirely because of self-interest.

I don't think that the issue is Fitzgerald's indifference to anthropology or to extracting ideas from observations. In 1929, while he was writing the Basil stories, he sent a letter to Sinclair Lewis congratulating him on the appearance of *Dodsworth*. Lewis's novel examined the way that the upper middle class lived—and Fitzgerald praised it precisely because it had revealed the "verity" of its coverage. In fact, he compared its characters to "dozens of people" he knew who were exactly like those in the novel.[37] So there was nothing intrinsically wrong in trying to discover "real American peoples." But there was a great deal wrong about critical conceptions. Fitzgerald's Mr. Utsonomia is flawless in one respect: he is scrupulously objective in his documentation of reality. Although he has the perfect critical mentality, reality evades him.

The last word is left to the narrator who states that data need interpretation. That is a motif in Fitzgerald, who in "How to Waste Material" had argued that Mencken's disciples—"insensitive, suspicious of glamour, preoccupied exclusively with the external, the contemptible, the 'national' and the drab"—wanted novels to be containers of "raw data" about American life. And novelists were only too glad to trade style for truism, "never sufficiently aware that material, however closely observed, is as elusive as the moment in which it has an existence."[38] The Basil stories (and many others in which Fitzgerald recalls the past) reconstruct historical moments. But they have in them important reflections on the use of data and conceptions, and especially of the methods of arriving at "verity." In Fitzgerald, "material" means more than subject.

The stories show how personality conflicts with community, an important topic in the 1920s and '30s. A contemporary of Fitzgerald, Henry A. Murray, who directed the Harvard Psychological Clinic at the same time that Fitzgerald began his Basil Duke Lee stories, spent much of his professional life working with fiction. Known especially for his work on Herman Melville,[39] Murray thought that evidence for American character should be sought in novels as well as in clinical studies. In the 1920s and '30s he wrote about identity as it was definitively formed by its social environment. Like Alfred North Whitehead, he was convinced that strictly scientific description would not reveal the true character of the experienced world. For Murray, individual relationships were driven by the unconscious as it had been described by Freud and Jung—and by the novels of Melville. In short, the mind was formed by its social experience while it agonistically resisted that experience. Murray turned to William James to explain the dynamics of the connection: "individuality is founded in feeling; and the recesses of feeling, the darker, blinder strata of character, are the only places in the world in which we catch real fact in the making, and directly perceive how events happen."[40]

Has Fitzgerald been aware of contemporary social theory? When Basil's headmaster tries to explain groups and individuals, he uses the language of diagnosis: "Among boys and masters there seemed to exist an extraordinary hostility toward him, and though Doctor Bacon had dealt with many sorts of schoolboy crimes, he had neither by himself nor with the aid of trusted sixth-formers been able to lay his hands on its underlying cause. It was probably no single thing, but a combination of things; it was most probably one of those intangible questions of personality."[41] Fitzgerald's passage indicates that this miniature social system has its own structure and rules. But there is more to the passage than the dynamics of intolerance. In the late 1920s "personality" was itself an embattled term. Psychologists like Edwin G. Boring wanted the discipline to have the hard scientific style (and the infallibility) of physics. For behaviorists, nothing about the mind was intangible. On the other hand, adversaries of the older system like Henry Murray thought that insights came from outside the laboratory. He hoped to work with "intellectuals at large" who had a "burning interest in human beings."[42] As Murray and newer minds looked at the issue, they accepted uncertainty. The concept of the indefinable separates Fitzgerald from the devotion of his mentors and directs us toward the theme of contradiction found often in his text.

Dr. Bacon is as hard-edged as any of Fitzgerald's characters who are governed by money and class. But he is having a representative moment. Fitzgerald's characters often address social ideas, state their views on social order, even identify what they have been reading. Dr. Bacon is more intellectually careful than most: Amory Blaine takes seriously the diagnostic value of physiognomy, a pseudo-science invalidated even as he ponders it; Mr. Utsonomia, who has modeled himself on social anthropology, takes sides in the current debate about corrupt cities versus noble provinces; in a time of racial troubles, Tom Buchanan imagines himself to be an arbiter of social conscience; Baby Warren (who needs a good deal of analysis) adopts the concept of class warfare to all of her human relations. And Dr. Bacon reminds us that social questions will not generate the answers we expect. Is that a surrender to indifference? A very few years earlier, in that other great book of 1925, *Science and the Modern World*, Alfred North Whitehead had stated that explanation is useless when most arbitrarily sure of observable fact. Ideas "may be expected to refer to depths beyond anything which we can grasp with a clear apprehension."[43] In short, he was deeply suspicious of explanation based upon supposedly objective evidence. Such references do more than clarify Fitzgerald's use of social science. They suggest his skepticism about ideas in a particular way. Even while his characters argue their social beliefs they are governed by what James called the blind strata of their character. They often mention what is on Fitzgerald's mind as well as on theirs. While we think of his stories imaging social history, they may also be defining society itself.

2

SOMETHING YOU KNOW ABOUT

In *The Beautiful and Damned* (1922) Adam and Anthony Patch debate writing in America. Apart from the fact that it is not a socially respectable career, Adam wants his shifty grandson at least to document the historical world accurately. The immediate problem is that Adam Patch confuses facts with truth, while Anthony Patch doesn't understand either:

> "I thought—it seemed to me that perhaps I'm best qualified to write—"
>
> Adam Patch winced, visualizing a family poet with long hair and three mistresses.
>
> "—history," finished Anthony.
>
> "History? History of what? The Civil War? The Revolution?"
>
> "Why—no, sir. A history of the Middle Ages." Simultaneously an idea was born for a history of the Renaissance popes, written from some novel angle. Still, he was glad he had said "Middle Ages."
>
> "Middle Ages? Why not your own country? Something you know about?"[1]

The secondary problem is larger. While Fitzgerald was planning *The Beautiful and Damned,* he wrote to Thomas Boyd using the same phrase that Adam Patch believes to be definitive, asking how readers can be expected to understand their "own country." The "detailed reporting" of social life failed, he said, because fiction was really an interpretation of facts.[2] That differs considerably from the view of Adam Patch and the literary faith he represents.

Fitzgerald wrote often about failed writers who, like Richard Caramel in *The Beautiful and Damned,* want to be both sentimental and "true to life."[3] In a letter to Max Perkins he said that their method was to show "the Great Beautiful Appreciation they have of the Great Beautiful life" of America, combining fake realism with fake romance.[4] And after discussion with Perkins, he had Scribner advertise *The Beautiful and Damned* as a study of "a section of American society which has never before been recognized as an entity—that wealthy, floating population which throngs the restaurants, cabarets, theatres and hotels of our great cities—people adrift on a sea of luxury, without the anchors of homes and the rudders of responsibilities—people without roots or background." The selling point was that the book was more informed than competing novels about "a significant phase of modern life."[5]

Those closest to Fitzgerald and his work admired his use of the social facts. Charles Scribner III stated that Fitzgerald's romantic imagination was expressed through "characters and settings."[6] Scottie Fitzgerald believed that her father was read because he knew American social history and "recorded it all." She resisted the idea that he was only the voice of the 1920s: "after you've read the stories, perhaps you'll ask yourself, as I did, 'Well, it's absorbing writing, but what's jazzy about it?'" Instead, she argued that his great subject was the way citizens lived between the world wars.[7] Sheilah Graham's *College of One* describes books that Fitzgerald gave her on European economics, history, and political science. Graham said of one book important to both of them, Morton's *A People's History of England,* that it "gives the complete story of England from the people's point of view, not from those above looking down. It gives the reasons for the formation of Parliament and the evolution of the bourgeoisie as a class." She added that "Morton—and Scott—went into great detail about the transformation of the working class."[8] For Max Perkins, the components of social reality in *The Great Gatsby*—"conversation" and "action"—provide its authority.[9]

According to Edmund Wilson, Christian Gauss, who taught both Wilson and Fitzgerald at Princeton, customarily dealt with "the assumptions, social, aesthetic and moral" of literature whether classic or romantic. In fact, Gauss usually accompanied discussions of the technique of art with "a highly developed sense of history."[10] Fitzgerald himself told interviewers that he owed much to social theory; later in life he wrote that Mark Twain was to be valued because he was the first writer who looked at American society objectively in order "to find out about men and how they lived together."[11]

It's reasonable to believe that Fitzgerald shared that interest. Matthew J.

Bruccoli wrote that Fitzgerald was a reliable social historian because he accurately invoked "the sense of time and place."[12] However, there were different understandings of the social subject. Each "science" had its own methodology. And while cultural anthropology was already familiar, sociology was just beginning to develop statistical data after the great population shifts caused by World War I. Sociology, "for the great majority in the 1920s . . . had become the study of human groups." It covered activities, education, employment, family, and leisure.[13] Fitzgerald alludes often to conventional divisions of class and to community, family, and local institutions. However, sociological explanation of these things in Fitzgerald has less authority—a lot less—than individual experience. His focus was always on the internal meaning of human relationships. William James's *A Pluralistic Universe* had reaffirmed in 1909 that the problem of knowing humans was not that of detecting social gradients but understanding individual variation.[14] Fitzgerald used concepts of social history and the language of social science throughout his work. The way he did this can be drawn from Santayana's essay on James in 1920: "personal human experience, expressible in literature and in talk, and no cosmic system however profound, was what James knew best and trusted most."[15]

Big treatises on Western culture by Marx, Freud, and Spengler were accompanied by new social studies that imitated laboratory science. They used statistics, interviews, and testing. So far, so good. But theory could be conjecture—while practice might not reproduce clinical conditions. We recall that Fitzgerald's stories are often about errors, prejudices, and obsessions about men and women. As transmitted to the public, social science could become ideology. We recognize some of the effects on Fitzgerald's characters:

- The pattern of social theory (Durkheim, Freud, Marx, Spengler, Toynbee) went from initial acceptance to enthusiasm to loss of belief when predictions failed. Isaiah Berlin's *The Sense of Reality* catalogs nineteenth-century systems that were abandoned because they confused "the sciences of social statics and social dynamics" (that wistful phrase is Herbert Spencer's) with quantitative science. Essentially, they had one answer to every problem and it failed in the application.[16]

- Fitzgerald's career exactly matches the rise of pseudosciences like eugenics and racialized biology. Richard Overy's *The Morbid Age* has an astonishing overview of intellectuals like H. G. Wells and Bernard Shaw who extracted from biology the pseudoidea of "decline" in body and mind. Images "of the social body assailed by disease and psychological disorder . . . remained the stock-in-trade of popular biological discourse."[17] Wells successfully marketed those ideas for the uncritical but literate middle class—comprising among others Harry Bellamy in "The Ice Palace."

- There were marketplace delusions like the books Tom Buchanan reads, the tabloid "philos'phy" that Amory Blaine repeats at the Knickerbocker Bar, and the midcult quackery recorded by Hemingway—"Our deepest convictions—will Science upset them? Our civilization—is it inferior to older orders of things?"—while reading the *Forum* magazine.[18] Nevertheless, innumerable lectures, pamphlets, best sellers, magazine articles, editorials, commercial courses, and radio talks marketed trends, truisms—and fallacies. "Try to explain social life," Walter Lippmann wrote in 1922: "the very fact that men theorize at all is proof that their pseudo-environments, their interior representations of the world, are a determining element in thought, feeling, and action."[19] He concluded that the behavior of other human beings was judged by the prejudices of the observer—and that even sociologists should never trust public opinions.

Fitzgerald described regnant concepts and some of them, exactly as experience shows, dwindle into fantasy and rationalization. He connects them to a social order existing in the mind of the beholder. The subject of "The Ice Palace" (1920) is not only character in the regressive South but also ideas in the progressive North. Harry Bellamy describes southerners as "sort of degenerates," and the phrasing indicates that he is trying to apply concept to subject.[20] Harry may have been reading Max Nordau on *Degeneration* (1892) although it is more likely that he found the book's ideas in recirculated form. Madison Grant's *The Passing of the Great Race* had been published in 1916; Lothrop Stoddard's *The Rising Tide of Color against White Supremacy* came out in 1920; the *Saturday Evening Post* carried essays by Kenneth Roberts throughout the 1920s about the eugenic dangers of immigration.[21] The idea of decline had been routinely applied to issues of everyday life. Infinitely elastic, it went from Darwinian morbidity to the absence of manners. Anxiety "over racial degeneration, both physical and moral" was "fuelled by alarmist reports" in the press.[22] There was always the need to act about some perceived deficiency, and magazine culture—as Hemingway noted of the *Forum*—was admonitory. Fitzgerald's rich boys, like Harry Bellamy, rarely sport with Amaryllis in the shade. They are industrious, busy defending established values, that is, using philosophies of the past to enforce rules. In Fitzgerald, plutocracy means power, privilege, and style—and also the obligation to protect status by doctrine. Like Tom Buchanan, rich boys see themselves manning the barricades of civilization. Like Braddock Washington, they are wardens of the middle class.

In "The Rich Boy," Anson Hunter defines himself through "family." Yet Lionel Trilling wrote that "our sense of family has become much attenuated." We have learned to think of the family "in dissolution" and while "this was once thought to be calamity . . . it is the natural course of things. We are sure that the nineteenth-century family was an elaborate hoax and against nature."[23] In Fitzgerald, "family" is a equivocal subject. We remember Tom Buchanan's constant use of the term: his default position is to invoke "family" whenever he wants someone else to do something, when he wants to protect himself, and when it is necessary to argue that his own usage is a part of natural law. His argument is part of that elaborate hoax.

Warren G. Harding's campaign speech of May 14, 1920, made the term "normalcy" a rubric of the times. He added a sustaining idea: clearly, normalcy could not be achieved without some form of cultural and perhaps even legislative "restoration." Both meanings argue that the present could not cross boundaries established in the past. Fitzgerald's most perceptive reviewer, Edmund Wilson, argued that his great accomplishment by 1922 was the *present-ness* of *The Beautiful and Damned*. He wrote that whenever Anthony and Gloria "come into contact with institutions, with the serious life of their times, these are made to appear ridiculous." Wilson concludes that the novel is about reaction to those structures and associations that define—and also camouflage—"organized society."[24]

Anson Hunter is one of those Fitzgerald characters who is formally allied with "organized society." He has enough money to imitate the splendid insouciance of Eustace Tilley who had just appeared on the first *New Yorker* cover. But Anson chooses instead to represent moral authority. The most central of his beliefs rests on "family" and "reversion" to the past. Why—exactly like Tom Buchanan—is he obsessed with obsolete social values? The separate stories of Anson's and Fitzgerald's other rich boys are part of another and larger story. For at least ten years, substantially before Fitzgerald had become a professional writer, H. L. Mencken had been arguing that human progress depended on patrician dominance: "the capital defect in the culture of These States is the lack of a civilized aristocracy, secure in its position, animated by an intelligent curiosity, skeptical of all facile generalizations, superior to the sentimentality of the mob, and delighting in the battle of ideas for its own sake."[25] In the early 1920s when Mencken loomed large, Fitzgerald believed that. His heroes want to be aristocratic exceptions to democratic banality. But by the time of *The Great Gatsby* and "The Rich Boy" he saw that it was far more useful writing about pretense. He had fewer illusions than Mencken, understanding that patrician culture was an imposition. It was self-satisfied, materialistic, and never in any danger of being "civilized." In fact, in 1926, at the same time "The Rich Boy" appeared, Walter Lippmann wrote that "a privileged elite" had to be judged by the same standards as "the popular culture." It could not disguise its motives by invoking "a family tree."[26]

Fitzgerald's rich families provide apologetics, and he invariably turns family history into a conflict of ideas. Parents and those who act for them are not simply blocking figures, heavy fathers from the stage. They have ideologies: hard-shell fundamentalists, recruiters for Comstock, true believers in tabloids, evangelical wowsers like John Granby in "The Perfect Life." They are boozers, chasers, senile, or functionally invisible like Anson Hunter's frigid uncle Robert or Jordan Baker's aunt who is about a thousand years old. They have a lot to say about class, race, immigration, national character. Their beliefs have an overpowering resemblance to the nativism embedded in the Prohibition movement.[27] They have the power of money over ideas: "this feeble, unintelligent old man was possessed of such power that, yellow journals to the contrary, the men in the republic whose souls he could not have bought directly or indirectly would scarcely have populated White Plains."[28] Yet the most important characteristic of the older generation in Fitzgerald is its intellectual absence from the present. Here is one of Fitzgerald's observations on that at the end of the decade of the 1920s: "Some generations are close to those that succeed them; between others the gap is infinite and unbridgeable. Mrs. Buckner—a woman of character, a member of Society in a large Middle-Western city—carrying a pitcher of fruit lemonade through her own spacious back yard, was progressing across a hundred years. Her own thoughts would have been comprehensible to her great-grandmother; what was happening in a room above the stable would have been entirely unintelligible to them both."[29] Fitzgerald managed the difficult feat of describing his own generation, the class of 1917, without mentioning parents or family. He states that a generation becomes conscious through a "reaction against the fathers which seems to occur about three times in a century."[30] The term "fathers" in that statement contains more than one meaning: a voice calls up from Braddock Washington's prison, "Hey! . . . you ain't goin' away without givin' us your blessing?"[31]

❋

Fitzgerald's work from 1919 on cited terms and ideas from social science. One of the most revealing passages is from a 1934 letter to V. F. Calverton, congratulating him on the publication of "The Passing of the Gods": "You are a modern Lecky and I congratulate you on the achievement . . . the synthesis of anthropology, sociology and philosophy, salted with good eighteenth rationalism, seems like a triumph."[32] Scott Donaldson says of this passage that it is meant to praise—and also to assert Fitzgerald's own intellectual independence. He did not share Calverton's faith in a Marxist future and was unwilling to discard his own empiricism.[33] Fitzgerald's evocation of disciplines confirms Sheilah Graham on his simultaneous use of literature and history. She emphasized politics; Mathew J. Bruccoli stated that his interest in literature was part of a general interest in intellectual history; Donaldson cited his understanding of economic probability and social structure in his own fiction.[34]

In "The Swimmers," Fitzgerald used categories of class and family to *begin* his explanation of behavior. In "Dalyrimple Goes Wrong" (1919), a working man is "listlessly struggling that losing struggle against mental, moral, and physical anemia that takes place ceaselessly on the lower fringe of the middle classes."[35] Fitzgerald did not let go of that thread; the rest of the story is a grown-up version of Basil Duke Lee's "The Captured Shadow," which describes the actual experience so badly contained by the phrase "downward social mobility." In *The Beautiful and Damned* (1922), Dot Raycroft lives the involuntary life of those not "born to a higher stratum" of the social order.[36] In "Winter Dreams" (1922), upward social mobility is always shadowed by its opposite. Dexter thinks of two things juxtaposed: where he is going, and what he has had to give up to get there. Everything in this story has its price, including identity.

The understood topic is always our social order—which, however, contains a great deal of social disorder. One of the most striking themes in Fitzgerald is the operation of ideas on those without them. It's possible to think of his work from the mid-1920s to the mid-1930s as if it were centered on "disturbed and antisocial behavior," but I think that cultural beliefs are more important than pathology.[37] What he calls the process of "absorbing culture" begins with print and ends in the minds of a "class, which makes up the so called upper class in every American city." The collective mind is dominated by conscience and sentiment and is always behind the times.[38] For example, Anson Hunter intends to judge social relations in the 1920s by standards he learned in 1910.

He is motivated by "a feeling that was more than personal, a reversion toward that family solidarity on which he had based his pride."[39] That seems simple but is an act of psychological faith. Santayana thought the concept of reversion had to be examined. In *The Life of Reason* (1905) he commented on the defensive habit, a kind of cultural tic, of appealing to the past in order to justify acts in the present. Ideas of the past were politically subjective, impossible to communicate to those with a different "human experience." Santayana linked the habit of invoking the past to religious apparitions, concluding that "to revert to primordial feeling is an exercise in mental disintegration."[40] That seems strongly worded until we recall the results of Anson Hunter's pietàs. And we begin to understand the mythopoeic relationship of great wealth and power to suffering and death in the Buchanan, Hunter, Warren, and Washington annals.

Fitzgerald avoided historical moralism. He loved the past, or part of it, but realized that the main subject of his work had to be transition between that past and an uncertain present. Sheilah Graham noticed that he was most interested in the "transformation" of the working class. That meant tracking the effects of both money and style. He was interested in change, not status. Thomas Piketty's *Capital* finds that both economics and literature share that view: "Even today, some people imagine, as Pareto did, that the distribution of wealth is rock stable, as if it were somehow a law of nature. In fact, nothing could be further from the truth. When we study inequality in historical perspective, the important thing to explain is not the stability of the distribution but the significant changes that occur from time to time."[41] When classes do change in Fitzgerald, they retain a sense of their past lives. For example, in *The Great Gatsby*, Myrtle Wilson is annoyed by "the shiftlessness of the lower orders," and Mrs. McKee tells Nick that an admirer was "way below me."[42] In order to protect the status they want, they attack their own past lives, put distance between themselves and old realities. Unlike Hemingway—*completely* unlike Hemingway—Fitzgerald's characters belong to family, class, and community and have to be understood within their social web. They identify their own standing and never stop interrogating the standing of other people. So we are always reminded that within a given scene the dimension of place is modified by the dimension of time.

The personal lives of Fitzgerald's characters can't be separated from their past or from American history. We see that in *The Great Gatsby* and throughout the stories. Sally Carrol Happer defends both the old and the new South in "The Ice Palace"; Henry Marston in "The Swimmers" finds it impossible to forget the men who came back from the Great War; Charlie Wales in "Babylon Revisited" thinks of being back in the Victorian past. Even Pat Hobby thinks about "the good old silent days" when you didn't need to read books in order to make movies of them.[43] It isn't nostalgia. The great study of global history by Jürgen Osterhammel concludes that the nineteenth century really did endure into the mind of the twentieth: it "did not end abruptly in August, 1914, before Verdun in 1916, or with Lenin's arrival at the Finland Station in Petrograd in April 1917. History is not a theatre where the curtain suddenly falls." Long into Woodrow Wilson's presidency, time present was understood to be part of "the world of yesterday."[44] We know that in *Middletown* the Lynds studied the 1920s by comparing schools, jobs, and domestic life to the 1890s. Fitzgerald himself wrote that when Hemingway satirized the year 1918 in his novel of 1929 he used standards of the lost world into which he had been born in 1899.[45] Scottie Fitzgerald wrote that she could never detect the themes of "Charleston" in her father's stories, "only the faint strumming of a latter-day 'Shine On, Shine On, Harvest Moon' or 'By the Sea, By the Sea, By the Beautiful Sea.'" She believed that those old songs and lyrics implied the emotional and historical range of her father's work.[46]

Fitzgerald was not alone when locating personality in history. In 1929, President Hoover commissioned a survey of American society based on the use of statistics. It was published in 1933 as *Recent Social Trends in the United States*. Robert S. Lynd did the section on consumers—which became a meditation about cash, credit, and civilization. Lynd began with a review of family income and expenditure but found that he had to think about the unresolved and "increasingly baffling" conflict between original and contemporary American character. He had to account for the preconditions of expenditure, which meant thinking about a new American culture that was individualistic, material, and secular. All of that could not be attributed to the replacement of cash by credit or, really, to the new ethic of consumption. According to Lynd, anyone depicting America in the 1920s had to start long before that time. The Puritan tradition still lingered, just enough to cause a kind of moral tension. He thought that it had ebbed not so much because of its inconvenient ethic but because, founded on a philosophy of hardship, of doing without, it no longer matched contemporary experience. The problem was that affluence was no cure for deprivation. Over "the past two decades" Americans had become wealthier and also insecure, lonely, bored to tears, and incapable of love. Lynd tried to connect the national state of mind to social conditions already described in *Middletown*: the incredible monotony of factory life, separation of individuals from family and community, and the disappearance of moral certainties within living memory.[47]

Fitzgerald was aware of these problems because a major part of his material came from "the past two decades." He was uncertain of theories of causation, more interested in observable behavior. The combination of economics and psychology used by John Maynard Keynes appeared in 1919: "I seek only to point out that the principle of accumulation based on inequality was a vital part of the pre-war order of Society and of progress as we then understood it, and to emphasize that this principle depended on unstable psychological conditions, which it may be impossible to recreate. It was not natural for a population, of whom so few enjoyed the comforts of life, to accumulate so hugely. The war has disclosed the possibility of consumption to all and the vanity of abstinence to many. Thus the bluff is discovered."[48] Keynes brought to public awareness three points of enormous importance. The first was that we could not return to conditions of the past. The second was that the current generation of great wealth—the playboy children of great inventors, builders, and financiers—had lost its nerve. The third is that the inheritors became apologists for a stable but entirely imaginary social order.[49] Fitzgerald is often adduced as a writer envious of or morally uncertain about wealth. That should be modified because he wrote about the attempt of wealth to justify itself, making great fiction out of social illusions.

The essential issue was the application of concepts to individual situations. Looking backward, Isaiah Berlin dismissed the great, groaning treatises that had dominated the imagination for so many years. He concluded that the real work of knowing society was done by those who put together "actual evidence" of human experience.[50]

As early as 1918, Fitzgerald was writing to Edmund Wilson and John Peale Bishop about evidence for describing individuals in groups. Bishop said that in his own case, reading Compton Mackenzie's *Youth's Encounter* "meant more to me now than it would have done at Princeton, but it has done more than all the sociology in the world. . . . This is undoubtedly the true, the undefiled aim of the novel—to present—but how shall I venture to speak to your ears, so fearful of banalities—any how it's not sociology."[51] If Bishop was right (and Fitzgerald's works strongly imply so), fiction was the métier for social understanding. And the past was the key to understanding the present. He could see the effect of experience on the individual mind. By examining social groups, he could follow values that were learned young and later rejected. The process of learning and rejection was one of his major patterns of thought.

3

THE OLD AMERICA

Fitzgerald's stories recover his own past and that of the country in its transformation from provincial to city life. Like that history, the stories are a disorderly progress, telling us how inherited ideas about social life failed to account for the way things were. It was not an easy project: "You see, I not only announced the birth of my young illusions in 'This Side of Paradise' but pretty much the death of them in some of my last Post stories like 'Babylon Revisited.'"[1] To judge by Fitzgerald's letters of the 1930s, he was almost as much concerned with the past as with the present. He studied his earlier work, and it would be a mistake to think that even the Basil Duke Lee stories for all their lightness of being are free of intense feeling about "the battles that engrossed us then."[2]

One part of the past was often on his mind: the old America that "passed away somewhere between 1910 and 1920."[3] Some of his stories take place at that time; while his characters of the 1920s and '30s have lived through it. The period was a magnet for recollection. Aside from the Basil Duke Lee stories there are Edmund Wilson's essays on the Hill School and Princeton—and there is a short, sharp memoir by Betty Ames, a Saint Paul friend of Fitzgerald who married Norris Jackson, a classmate at Princeton: "From the 1900s until the first world war was a special, happy time to be young. The tone of the time was much simpler than nowadays. It was all before the first World War and the whole temper of the United States was entirely different. People had no idea there [were] going to be those holocausts. There was constantly dances, and the debutante life—you really wouldn't believe it. It was a mass of teas, luncheons, receptions, dances, and parties. It's really side-splitting now to think of having lived through that."[4] Fitzgerald recalled in 1939 that his generation had in fact "inherited two worlds—the one of hope to which we had been bred; the one of disillusion which we had discovered early for ourselves."[5] Edmund Wilson admired the national past but realized that it had become unreachable. Here is the ending of his 1942 memoir for Alfred Rolfe, his teacher at Hill School: "Suddenly, as I write this memoir, it seems to me that the stream he was following flowed out of a past that is now remote: from Emerson with his self-dependence, and *The Wonderful One-Hoss Shay* with its satire on the too-perfect Calvinist system; from the days when people went to Germany to hear Wagner and study Greek; from Matthew Arnold, from Bernard Shaw—now almost an old-fashioned classic like Arnold. And I am glad to renew my sense of Alfred Rolfe's contribution to it, as I realize that I myself have been trying to follow and feed it at a time when it has been running low. Its tradition antedates our Christian religion and has in many men's minds survived it, as one may hope it will, also, the political creeds, with their secular evangelism, that are taking the Church's place."[6] Wilson went back to 1909; George Orwell's recollection of his own education in 1911 makes a different point: "I did not question the prevailing standards, because so far as I could see there were no others. . . . And yet from a very early age I was aware of the impossibility of any *subjective* conformity."[7] He came to the issue much earlier than Wilson or Fitzgerald. Lionel Trilling's essay on Orwell states that he was "declassed" along with other intellectuals who "broke" with prevailing conceptions of social order.[8] Judgments about the era came from interested parties who are after all retelling their own lives as if they were portraits of Western culture. However, the mountain of nineteenth-century scholarship summarized by Jürgen Osterhammel concludes that what happened "before 1914" really was as important as the Great War itself. The high middle class would disintegrate because "activities, lifestyles, and mentalities" defined identity in a way that status never could.[9] Basil Duke Lee is fifteen, one of those mentalities recognizing "a world much larger and more brilliant than themselves that existed outside their windows and beyond their doors."[10] The war is years away.

Fitzgerald's metaphors of war and death imply more than sexual rebellion in the Jazz Age. Sheilah Graham recalled that Fitzgerald did have a larger subject: "the reality of living human beings—men and women who in their time had toiled over manuscripts and hunted an elusive world." Her account of her own reading includes that of Fitzgerald who had written on the margin of his "Eve of St. Agnes," "you'll see where Keats got his idea for these lines."[11] I take that to mean his sources for the story—and also the enabling conception Keats drew from a culture that had sufficed for six hundred years. He emphatically told Sheilah that writers needed a sense of historical and also philosophical authority.

Yet the most familiar metaphor Fitzgerald used is "the authority of failure." It has usually been interpreted as self-description, although William Troy (1945) thought that the more arresting part of the phrase was *authority*. Troy was not grateful to the critics recently featured in *The Crack-Up* because they defined failure as Fitzgerald's inability to produce books they wanted to read. They were moralistic, implying that his sensibility dominated his work. Troy cut through that issue: failure was a subject, not a state of mind. *The Beautiful and Damned* (1922) "is not so much a study in failure as in the *atmosphere* of failure—that is to say, of a world in which no moral decisions can be made because there are no values in terms of which they may be measured."[12] It was not a great novel, but it showed that good writers see the connection between states of being and what is deceptively called social order.

States of being are often attributed to war and social change, or to the lag between tradition and technology, or to insufficient political ideas. Fitzgerald was accused of failing to treat such matters, and Troy wholeheartedly thanked him for ignoring that advice. War and politics are mentioned in Fitzgerald, but they are never necessary causes of anything. In fact, they are effects. Fitzgerald wrote about experience. The Troy essay ends with a remark overheard: "'It's under you, over you, and all around you,' he protested, in the hearing of the present writer, to a young woman who had connived [sic] at the slow progress of his work. 'And the problem is to get hold of it somehow.' It was exasperating because for the writer, whose business is to extract the unique quality of his time . . . there was too much to be sensed, to be discarded, to be reconciled into some form of order."[13] That is one reason why the past matters so greatly in Fitzgerald; it is evidence experienced.

The recollections with which I began are, famously, about schools— Fitzgerald on the Newman School, Wilson on the Hill School, Orwell on Saint Cyprian's. Yet formal schooling was only a beginning. Many of Fitzgerald's stories take the form of a later and unwilling education. Freud's *Civilization and Its Discontents*, written at the same time (1929) as Fitzgerald's stories about Basil Duke Lee, locates the beginning of discontent in false innocence: "that the education of young people at the present day conceals from them the part which sexuality will play in their lives is not the only reproach which we are obliged to make against it. Its other sin is that it does not prepare them for the aggressiveness of which they are destined to become the objects. In sending the young out into life with such a false psychological orientation, education is behaving as though one were to equip people starting on a Polar expedition with summer clothing and maps of the Italian Lakes."[14] Freud adds ironically, "a certain misuse is being made of ethical demands." That takes in much more than sexual rebellion—and it seems to have been understood by Eleanor in *This Side of Paradise* (1920). She says, "I'm hipped on Freud and all that," describing Catholic education as "just all cloaks, sentiment and spiritual rouge and panaceas." Amory also knows Freud and states that the problem is more inclusive: our whole intellectual past became "diluted with Victorian sentiment."[15] That ought to be linked to Freud's conception of aggressiveness because *sentiment* (unlike *sentimentality*) is a quality enforced.

A particular kind of sentiment recurs in Fitzgerald. In a 1940 letter to his daughter he recalls that at Princeton there had not been any connection between assigned reading and "explanations" of it.[16] He was required not only to see the text as others did but also to replicate their late Victorian enthusiasm for rhymed emotion. In *This Side of Paradise*, Amory is described in a poetry class, and while the lecture on Swinburne and Tennyson drones on, he scribbles a response: "*Thousands of old emotions / And a platitude for each.*" Yet Amory's class is not entirely about lyrics. His instructor is plainly in love with Victorian stability, and the lecture turns out to be a celebration of idealized social "order." It is the larger subject. Amory has been thinking about his own contempt for Tennyson "and all he stood for." That is quickly defined: "*Answers to life in rhyme.*"[17]

Sentiment denotes emotionalized thought, and according to Mencken it extended itself into a range of meanings. He was especially interested in the way it ruled social life. Mencken's essay on "Forbidden Words" in *The American Language* describes the age of euphemism after the Civil War. Restraints on language were not confined to the human body or to sexuality, and he concluded that *anything* could be controversial. Subjects could not be introduced, discussed, or evaluated. Even Hollywood, with "its own Index Expurgatorius," repressed scripts that dealt with socially unacceptable—or even disagreeable—facts.[18] His point, like Fitzgerald's, was not that indecency had to be repressed but that intellectual inquiry had to be repressed. In short, while Fitzgerald was aware that Keats had inherited ideas fit to frame his discourse he could not say the same for himself. His stories repeatedly portray characters without cultural ideas sufficient for their agency. The "answers" they get for life are demonstrably wrong. The text of "Spires and Gargoyles" is explicit: "instinctive" life is opposed to the "age" and its "environment."[19] That formulation shadows Fitzgerald's dramatic action.

The wrong answers insistently impose themselves. George Herbert Mead's *Mind, Self, and Society* (1934) used the phrase "social control" to describe ideas enforced by community on the individual. Mead wrote that the process was benign—although it was so "intimately and extensively" experienced that it could hardly be rejected. He admitted that enforced ideas might turn out to be entirely wrong when historically judged.[20] A few years later, John Dewey described new social character encumbered by old social values: "But it is useless to bemoan the departure of the good old days . . . if we expect by bemoaning and exhortation to bring them back. It is radical conditions which have changed, and only an equally radical change in education suffices. We must recognize our compensations—the increase in toleration, in breadth of social judgment, the larger acquaintance with human nature, the sharpened alertness in reading signs of character and interpreting social situations, greater accuracy of adaptation in differing personalities, contact with greater commercial activities. These considerations mean much to the city-bred child of today."[21]

American philosophy had for some time been concerned with the problem of beliefs that had outlived their usefulness. From 1911 on, George Santayana had published a series of essays on "Gentility," which, he said, began as a set of devout Protestant beliefs and ended as a set of trivial social observances. His first essay, "The Genteel Tradition in American Philosophy," described the American thinking classes from late Victorian times to the period described by Fitzgerald in the Basil stories. The last essay, "The Genteel Tradition at Bay," appeared in 1931, approximately when the Basil and Josephine stories were published. There are consistent themes in the sequence, beginning with the premise that "hereditary philosophy has gone stale." Santayana developed his argument from the point of view of the younger generation to whom "traditional mentality" had become an obstacle. However, it was conventional and to be obeyed—although it was also "secretly despised."[22] Santayana ended his sequence by repeating that "sentiment" had replaced functional "conscience." That undermined character; in fact, it made virtue dubious. Santayana used metaphors of natural decline and decay as opposed to the (moderately) healthy materialism of the current thinking generation.[23] Unlike midcult guardians of manners and morals, he posited credible opposition to the past. The first essay on "Gentility" took the form of a university lecture within which Santayana encouraged undergraduates to develop his ideas in their own professional work. The ending of "The Genteel Tradition at Bay" states that "tradition" around 1920 often takes the form of "groundless sentiment." But no one, until they become embarrassed by reality, realizes that tradition has to be modified: "Those who have lived in Boston—and who else should know?—are aware how earnestly the reformed New England conscience now disapproves of its disapprovals . . . if directed by sentiment only, and not by a solid science of human nature, conscience will always be pointing in a different direction."[24]

When Edmund Wilson wrote (literally) about the American scene, he provided a sense of history through biography. The narrator of I Thought of Daisy and Daisy herself are leaving the waxworks exhibits of the Eden Musée at Coney Island. They have passed through scenes of the previous world—which is to say their own early lives—leaving behind Brigham Young, Grant, Booker T. Washington, and other figures once well understood. The last of the exhibits no longer means anything:

> On our way out, I caught a glimpse of Roosevelt, the Teddy Roosevelt of San Juan Hill, who, with his handkerchief knotted about his neck, his Rough-Rider puttees, his felt hat, his moustache, his glaring teeth, and his eye-glasses, made me think of that younger America which I had assumed we had for ever left behind, but which today seemed quite close to me again. It had been a boy's America—and not merely because it had been the America of my boyhood. Roosevelt, who had been so charming with his children, had become the idol of Americans of that time for very much the same reasons—he had been everything that a boy could imagine: Dan Beard, Old and Young King Brady, Frank Merriwell, and Stanley in Africa, all rolled into one. I asked Daisy whether she remembered the time when Roosevelt had been a great hero. She said, "No,"—and showed so little interest that for a time I relapsed into silence.[25]

❀

In an unpublished foreword for Taps at Reveille, Fitzgerald stated: "before the last of these stories were written the world that they represented passed. In consequence the reviewer may be tempted to apply the title harshly to the fate of the collection. Yet almost all these stories, the winnowing of fifty odd, meant a great deal to the author at the time of the writing: all of them tried for an arduous precision in trying to catch one character or one emotion or one adventure—which is all that one can do in the length of a short story."[26] The "precision" of these stories begins with depiction of acts, events, and states of mind. I think that it extends necessarily to ideas pretending to explain experience.

The Basil Duke Lee stories were heavily represented in this collection. They originally appeared in the *Saturday Evening Post* from 1928 to 29; while the Josephine Perry stories appeared in the *Post* from 1930 to 1931. Fitzgerald planned to republish these sequences in a separate volume; however, he concluded in 1934 that "it would require a tremendous amount of work and a good deal of new invention to make them presentable."[27] The book project was abandoned, although five of the Basil stories became part of *Taps at Reveille* (1935). Fitzgerald's biographers have adduced a number of reasons for Fitzgerald's persistent recovery of the past. Matthew J. Bruccoli writes that Scott and Zelda both went through intense "self-assessment" at the end of the 1920s recorded in their conversation, letters, and works.[28] Bruccoli suggested that such self-judgment is necessarily a stage of a writer's life. Fitzgerald particularly needed to redefine his sense of self, because after *The Great Gatsby* he had failed to produce an influential, money-making novel.[29] He needed to reinforce the public sense of his importance as well as his own sense of competence. There are other essentials in the matrix of these stories.

The biographies contend that the Basil stories retell Fitzgerald's early life. But those stories are ambiguous. Their historical reconstruction provides a setting for critical thought. First, they comment on disparities of American culture before the 1920s; second, they are as ambiguous as the accounts by Wilson and Orwell that I have mentioned. Like the early Fitzgerald, Basil is naive and arrogant, responsible for his own disappointments at school, after school, and in love. His reflections on that are not shaped by native sources— even though Fitzgerald was a scholar of literature about growing up. One constant in the Basil stories is conflict between personality and moral authority—a theme also of the flapper stories. That theme is often stated by Freud in his general reflections on culture. To a surprising extent, Freud read marketplace texts. He found sentimental novels to be as useful as writing of a much heavier caliber, and in letters, reviews, and essays, he wrote about the literature of escapism, especially stories about rising in the world and changing inner identity. Here is Freud in 1923 on conflict between the individual and culture: "as a child grows up, the role of father is carried on by teachers and others in authority; their injunctions and prohibitions remain powerful in the ego ideal and continue, in the form of conscience, to express the moral censorship . . . experienced as a sense of guilt."[30] That should alert us to Fitzgerald's repeated use of education as a setting for the coercion of ideas.

Fitzgerald's choice of "battle" as a term to describe social values was appropriate. The Basil stories recall the injunctions, limitations, and penalties of culture. Even a kiss has a philosophy: "What was the implication—that kissing people was all right, was even admirable? He remembered what John Granby had said: 'Every time you kiss a nice girl you may have started her on the road to the devil.'"[31] A kiss doesn't appear to be much of a casus belli, but it had representative power.[32] This one even has a provenance. Anthony Comstock, according to Mencken, was known for his diatribe against arousing "a libidinous passion . . . in the mind of a modest woman."[33] Anthony Comstock Patch in *The Beautiful and Damned* has been named after him and Adam J. Patch, his grandfather, is a convert to "Comstockery." The term implied more than personal morality. In *Prejudices: Second Series* (1921), Mencken described the disastrous effect on American *intellectual* life caused by "the whole complex of social and political attitudes underlying Prohibition—the whole clinical picture of Puritanism rampant."[34] Before that book appeared, Fitzgerald wrote to him saying that he, John Peale Bishop, and Edmund Wilson had "read most of the essays" in their original form. By 1920, Fitzgerald had already formulated his position: in a letter to the *Princeton Alumni Weekly* he wrote that outworn values were "camouflaged under the name of 'social service'" and "had little connection with modern life and modern thought."[35] The great American problem was not vice but virtue.

Fitzgerald's novel sardonically names those deviations—art, theater, literature—that are the real targets of Adam's "reform." We now think of the 1920s as a decade of liberation, although those who lived through the decade resented social interference in personal and public life. There were a number of reasons for thinking about daily experience as a "battle." Its events were witnessed, judged, and penalized. Prohibition absorbed Comstockery as well as other forms of public morality so that the war on alcohol that began by defending the values of sobriety became a political coalition. Lisa McGirr describes its merger with "the earlier reform ethos" promoted by schools and other institutions of community life, by evangelicalism, and even by the Progressive movement. It was the fate of all public morality insisting on "social cohesion and moral regulation" to be rejected. She concludes that Prohibition ended not only with the repeal of legislation on drinking but with the establishment of a new national consensus on "individual rights, tolerance, and pluralism."[36]

During its reign Comstockery converted the events of private life into in-fractions against public life. Comstock believed that independence led to sex-ual depravity while flappers—especially Fitzgerald's—believed that whatever depravity might be, it led to independence. "The extreme demands of Pro-hibition were a kind of last straw for American women, who used the wider cultural rebellion against Prohibition as a[n] opportunity to reject their moral subjugation in all its forms."[37] The point about Prohibition was it that wanted petrified social codes more than it wanted sobriety. John Dewey stated in 1930 that values learned in 1910 could never apply to experience acquired af-ter 1919. As to the pieties of Prohibition, "Dewey argued that the only hope was to bring out the *latent* order and reasonableness of modern society. . . . What held things up was not a deep and worsening crisis . . . but the clogging effect of traditional values." He blamed "blind tradition" for modern prob-lems rather than deviations from public morality.[38] At the same time, Lio-nel Trilling wrote that mental dysfunction was in fact "a collection of values" inherited from the past.[39] And Fitzgerald was going back into the unusable past with his stories about Basil and Josephine who were bound to a social contract they had never signed.

The stories show how those "stale" ideas named by Santayana affected stu-dents, flappers, soldiers, wage earners, the unemployed—and how they were used by rich boys and other moralists. "May Day" (1919) covers sources of belief in detail, from Edith Bradin's library of "current expressions, bits of journalese and college slang" to broadcasts, magazines, and "the scribes and poets" of advertising.[40] The mob gets its ideas indirectly, from rumors, soap-box speeches—even from Peter Himmel's bent social conscience. However, Fitzgerald, like Mencken, does not accuse masscult of destroying our cultural inheritance. He understood that "tabloids and the movies" cited by Mencken recycled old beliefs.[41] It became easier to absorb sentiment and conscience. In *The Great Gatsby*, Tom Buchanan is motivated by "stale ideas" of the genteel tradition. He is not especially concerned about radicalism. Although worried about the extinction of the sun and of the white race, he spends an enormous amount of time talking about manners, marriage, and social class. He argues from a particular point of view and about a particular subject: standards are values. He does not imply that there should be no adultery, only that adultery needs to be respectably conducted.

Fitzgerald consistently refers to the unusable American past in dialogues dealing with social conscience. Jobena Dorsey in "The Perfect Life" has dis-covered that "righteous men" and "upright young men" hide their motives behind Victorian respectability. She understands that the concept of "perfect lives" is not only unattainable but also a form of camouflage for imperfect lives.[42] In "The Jelly-Bean" (1920), the old culture actually withers away, and one of the great tropes of the story is its movement toward entropy. There are signposts, just as there are in *The Great Gatsby*, provided by the imagery of books: "Over Tilly's Garage, a bleak room echoed all day to the rumble and snorting down-stairs and the singing of the Negro washers as they turned the hose on the cars outside. It was a cheerless square of a room, punctuated with a bed and a battered table on which lay half a dozen books—Joe Miller's *On a Slow Train through Arkansas*; *Lucille*; in an old edition very much annotated in an old-fashioned hand; *The Eyes of the World* by Harold Bell Wright; and an ancient prayer-book of the Church of England with the name Alice Powell and the date 1831 written on the fly-leaf."[43] We think of the books that Alexis de Tocqueville found everywhere on the frontier, books that asserted recognizable intellectual strength and a powerful sense of the individual *ethos* in history.[44] Then there is that subtitle of the annotated *Lucille: A Story of the Heart: A Pathetic Domestic Drama in Three Acts*. All duly enacted in Fitzgerald. The adjectives deploy themselves around age and inertia, and I note that Santayana established some of the grand metaphors of his time even before 1920. As he put it, the roots of the past had withered and the social organism had died. But the dead wood was still there.

In "The Jelly-Bean," contemporary themes of work, success, and money are invoked; even the return to a place in local history for Jim Powell. He has been briefly energized by love before being derailed by the news of Nancy Lamar's marriage. Jim has no blueprint for creating his own life. And how could he? Mencken, who was the arbiter of ideas on the subject, suggested that there were no modern social concepts in the South: "The southerner . . . is a pleasant fellow—hospitable, polite, good-humored, even jovial. . . . But a bit absurd. . . . A bit pathetic."[45] In order for him to think his way out of misery he needs exactly what the South does not have, a secular tradition of "inquiry," a channel of "public opinion," and at least some "urbanity" in order to make comparisons. Georgia, according to Mencken, did not allow any individual "impulse" to change the conditions of southern life. Because of that, social change was impossible.[46] He argued that the only way out of the impasse was to escape, leaving the South behind exactly as history had done. The theme of escape (and pervasively, of thwarted escape) is built in to Fitzgerald's Tarleton stories. In three of them there is an expedition to the North, the experience of failure there, and finally the (ambiguous) resumption of southern identity. As in Mencken, the sequence dramatizes social history, and also true to Mencken, it begins with energy and ends with inertia.

Fitzgerald recognized that styles as much as rules determined social standards. When Marjorie in "Bernice Bobs Her Hair" says that *Little Women* has gone out of style, she is as definitive as Santayana, at least for her audience and in her time. Yet Marjorie is not all style. Like Fitzgerald's Dalyrimple she has been twice-born. At about the same historical moment, they both realize that standards do not change as quickly as events happen. Social life becomes a rather difficult and complex game of chess because no one really knows which standards apply to actions—or even if any standards apply. Sometimes there are complete reversals of social assumptions, as in Fitzgerald's crime stories. Edmund Wilson thought that there was a masking effect in such stories derived from their great original: "Dickens had invested his plots with a social and moral significance that made the final solution of the mystery a revelatory symbol of something that the author wanted seriously to say."[47] The real subject of crime stories was social order between the world wars.

Basil in "The Captured Shadow" has been thinking about "crook comedies" on Broadway. Like other things on his and Fitzgerald's minds, they have a late Victorian pedigree going back to "Alias Jimmy Valentine" by O. Henry and *Raffles* by E. W. Hornung. Stories about gentlemen crooks before the war turned out to have second lives not only on stage but also in magazines, novels, pulps, and especially movies. Film versions of the O. Henry story appeared in 1910, 1915, and 1928. And the genre did nothing but gain popularity from Douglas Fairbanks to Cary Grant. Orwell wrote in the early 1940s that it was immensely important because, if for no other reason, *Raffles* had become "one of the best-known characters in English fiction." Orwell also thought that whether or not crime paid, most of the interest in the story was aroused by social standing. At best, being middle class was invidious: "*Raffles*, no less than *Great Expectations* or *Le Rouge et le Noir*, is a story of snobbery, and it gains a great deal from the precariousness of Raffles's social position. A cruder writer would have made the 'gentleman burglar' a member of the peerage, or at least a baronet. Raffles, however, is of upper-middle-class origin and is only accepted by the aristocracy because of his personal charm. 'We were in Society but not of it,' he says to Bunny towards the end of the book."[48] The Raffles story showed the middle class enacting its resentments, but it also offered a much larger theme to Fitzgerald, that of maintaining one's class, let alone transcending it.

Fitzgerald's own gentleman burglar, Bryan Dalyrimple, is a returned war hero who finds that nothing on the home front matters as much as money. He runs out of money and has to work in the stockroom of the Theron G. Macy Company—which is as "depressing" as Fitzgerald's unique prelude describes. It has been architecturally designed by H. G. Wells: underground for as much as fourteen hours a day, men in the basement have lost their human identity. They work like blundering machines in the "echoing half-darkness." There is never enough light to see anything clearly in this suffocating story, and Dalyrimple is shown trying always to climb out, breathe air, get to the horizon. Why is he there? At the heart of Dalyrimple's silent dialogues with himself is a verdict: "the old childhood principles" (which are all he knows) don't refer to social realities. He concludes that faithfulness has nothing to do with success, evil is rarely punished, virtue is never rewarded, honest poverty is less happy than corrupt wealth. That reverses the conventional oppositions of film and fiction—and also of the curriculum. *Middletown* soon provided an illustration. Here is the good social life as portrayed by instructions from the city to its teachers: "'The most fundamental impression a study of history should leave on the youth of the land when they have reached the period of citizenship,' begins the section and history and civics of the Middletown Course of Study of the Elementary Schools, 'is that they are their government's keepers as well as their brothers' keepers in a very true sense. This study should lead us to feel and will that sacrifice and service for our neighbor are the best fruits of life; that reverence for law, which means, also, reverence for God, is fundamental to citizenship; that private property, in the strictest sense, is a trust upon us to be administered for the public good; that no man can safely live unto himself."[49] Fitzgerald's story suggests that early ideas taught to him— "they told me"—were valedictory but untrue. That is not the half of it. Dalyrimple sees that "the sentimental a priori forms of his own mind" have been reinforced and even created by social fictions.[50] The theme of self-creation is central to Jay Gatsby's story. But so is the countertheme of Daisy Buchanan's story, the replacement of the ego by its culture. Fitzgerald's most disquieting narratives are about giving up the powers of consciousness, disappearing into silence. Dalyrimple does get out of that stockroom, which is not only an ascent but a rebirth. Yet his story raises other issues.

Those cover more than money. *The Transformation of the World* states that between 1900 and 1920 being part of the middle class meant having a sense of self: "ambition is not just a matter of personal ascent, family prosperity, and a perception of direct class interest." Being middle class means shaping events, and indeed in having a unique identity. Such a belief was stronger then,

Osterhammel writes, than *"any other nonreligious system of values."*[51] That is the burden of Fitzgerald's thought on his own situation, refracted in many essays, remarks, and letters about his obligations. In his life, he had what he called a passionate belief in order. In his work, he shows its fate. In this story, the most dispiriting consequence is the cancellation of identity. The "crook" story became relatively harmless and even somewhat saccharine when Basil tried his hand at it in "The Captured Shadow." There is no wonder that his deeply respectable audience found it entertaining without being threatening. But earlier versions of the story about Dalyrimple and Jay Gatsby show holes between social classes that are deep enough to fall into and disappear. In these stories, the self has to be created without its most authoritative support, past knowledge adequate to present experience.

4

COMPLEX FORTUNE

In Fitzgerald, those who are born to money have the power to direct the lives of other people. He observed that at home in Saint Paul, visiting Chicago, attending Princeton. The insight has been confused with the envy of wealth: Hemingway ridiculed his interest in the rich, and Edmund Wilson complained that he did not see deeply into their minds. Yet neither Hemingway nor Wilson ever explained why wealth was essential to his imagination—and to his portrayal of America. Fitzgerald was certainly interested in money—even more interested in the effects of money on personality and on our culture.

His understanding of the rich only began with purchasing power. He was a student of novels describing the relationship of inherited and acquired wealth. One of the great accounts of nineteenth-century fiction opposes a "received and prized conception of a hierarchical society securely based on land income" to "an emerging new society based on commercial and industrial income."[1] In fiction and in life, amounts of wealth were balanced against kinds of wealth. Yet there is more to Fitzgerald than the opposition between old and new money. His characters calculate their place in the social hierarchy. Ideas about social class are connected to their sense of developing selves. By the time we see them as adults they, like Fitzgerald, have lived through more than one economy—and its regime of ideas.

Inequality of income is instrumental in his work and in the most important novels about money of the past two centuries. It is not preeminent. However, we do have to begin with inequality since it serves as demarcation. Thomas Piketty's recent *Capital* is especially helpful because it argues persuasively that nineteenth-century novels are reliable sources of monetary evidence. In order to establish a baseline for middle-class expenditures in the nineteenth century, Piketty uses sums of annual expenses described by *Sense and Sensibility* and incomes derived from earnings and inheritance in *Père Goriot*. He finds unequal income to be the province of the novel from Balzac until at least 1920: "inequality of ownership of capital was somewhat less extreme in the New World. Clearly, this does not mean that American society in 1900–1910 embodied the mythical idea of an egalitarian society of pioneers. In fact, American society was already highly inegalitarian, much more than Europe today, for example. One has only to reread Henry James or note that the dreadful Hockney who sailed in luxury on *Titanic* in 1912 existed in real life and not just in the imagination of James Cameron to convince oneself that a society of rentiers existed not only in Paris and London but also in turn-of-the-century Boston, New York, and Philadelphia. . . . Income inequality increased quite sharply in the United States during the 1920s."[2] Disparate income in the novel led to the more central concern of fiction with the style and strategy of social life.

The general economic problem for the middle class was not as Mr. Pickwick put it, matching expenditure to income. In *Capital*, at least, the problem appears to have been paying the costs of middle-class style. "In the absence of modern technology, everything is very costly and takes time and above all staff. Servants are needed to gather and prepare food (which cannot easily be preserved). Clothing costs money: even the most minimal fancy dress might cost several months' or even years' income. Travel was also expensive. It required horses, carriages, servants to take care of them, feed for the animals, and so on. The reader is made to see that life would have been objectively quite difficult for a person with only 3–5 times the average income." If you wanted books or musical instruments or other indicators of success "there was no choice but to have an income 20–30 times the average of the day."[3] Even after 1900, earned income in Europe and America rarely covered such costs. It was especially difficult to cover the long-term cost of education, a subject reiterated in Fitzgerald's letters. That was not because such income was unavailable but because it was subject to variation.

According to Piketty only a few entrepreneurs throughout the nineteenth century equaled the annual income of rentiers. There is room for dispute on this point because the European and American economies were not identical. A drastic change occurred on this side of the Atlantic after the Civil War when manufacturing profits created raw wealth. Fitzgerald wrote often about the new social chessboard after 1870. Some of his characters get rich from mining or manufacturing, and the money they make later becomes a vast system of inheritances. He is much more interested in how the second generation uses that money than in how the first generation obtains it. Fitzgerald focused on the way that new money positioned itself as a new form of aristocracy.[4] A current history of economics states of the period after 1870 that "first- and second-generation bourgeois potentates had just sprung from social obscurity and the homeliest economic pursuits. . . . As their social prominence and economic throw weight increased at an extraordinary rate . . . so too did the need to fabricate delusions of stability and tradition, to feel rooted somehow even in the shallowest of soils, to thicken the borders of their social insulation." Ward McAllister originated "the four hundred" but had to admit that money alone would never be enough to secure deference in America: "so we have to draw social boundaries on another basis: old connections, gentle breeding . . . elegant leisure . . . count for more than newly gotten riches."[5] Fitzgerald writes about the effect of such upper-class pretension in his own time. He is skeptical not only about wealth itself but also about the daily effects it generates. Specifically, he writes about concepts of friendship, family, and love changed at will by the power of money. To see Tom Buchanan lecturing on "family" is to realize that this dunce has the power to change its definition and to make his fantasies into custom and law.

The novel from Balzac to Wharton identified the most desirable assets in financial and also in moral ways. Dependable sources were (relatively) risk free. However, even prudent investment could be dangerous. In the Victorian novel, land management and bonds gave low-yield profits, but that was not a reason to pursue wage earnings instead. It was a reason to get more land and bonds. That underlies not only the concept of investment but also of marriage. Any idea about the opposition of old and new money has to be balanced by a different idea, that of acceptable risk. There are good reasons why accountants and lawyers in Trollope play such large roles in the bumpy process from love to marriage—and why there are so many choices between marrying up for status and marrying down for dowry.

One of the great passages in American literature on conscientious investment is Fitzgerald's description of Nick's books on banking and credit at the beginning of *The Great Gatsby*. That gorgeous, golden shelf signifies accountable growth as well as profitability. The bonds that Nick sells are not intended for a quick turnover, nor are they intended for clients like the shady Walter Chase who is situated allegorically between Meyer Wolfshiem and

Tom Buchanan. Even Jay Gatsby, a crooked broker, has been brought up on "improving" books that argue that making money is part of making social selves. That can be seen in R. H. Tawney, whose *Religion and the Rise of Capitalism* appeared in the same year as Fitzgerald's "The Rich Boy"—and also in Horatio Alger, who is embedded in the Fitzgerald canon. Carl Bode states in his edition of *Ragged Dick* that Alger never conceived of rags to riches; his subject was rags to respectability. Alger's novels. according to Bode, quite literally preached "a Protestant ethic" by rewarding virtue with happiness.[6] Santayana's *Character and Opinion in the United States* (1920) stated that "the almighty dollar" was much less important to Americans than its signification of "success" as accomplishment.[7] It was extremely difficult to fit inheritance into this model. Even Anthony Patch who is born to millions is constantly urged to find employment that will validate him.

Status was interesting to the novel—but not as much as changes of status. *Capital* states that the coming of World War I brought a new dispensation of taxes and rising costs. Fixed returns declined. Wages increased and seemed to have equaled rentier income. Those conditions made the story of wealth more interesting because it was connected to contemporary fears. Fitzgerald begins his narrative of American economic history just before that change. *The Economic Consequences of the Peace* by Keynes offers a shrewd analysis of the circumstances. It contains a narrative more compelling than the primal story of accumulating wealth: "We are thus faced in Europe with the spectacle of an extraordinary weakness on the part of the great capitalist class, which has emerged from the industrial triumphs of the nineteenth century, and seemed a very few years ago our all-powerful master. The terror and personal timidity of the individuals of this class is now so great, their confidence in their place in society and in their necessity to the social organism so diminished, that they are the easy victims of intimidation. This was not so in England twenty-five years ago, any more than it is now in the United States. Then the capitalists believed in themselves, in their value to society, in the propriety of their continued existence in the full enjoyment of their riches and the unlimited exercise of their power. Now they tremble before every insult."[8] Keynes was a best seller, and some of his points resurfaced in the writings of Edmund Wilson and H. L. Mencken. Fitzgerald puts his own capitalists in a shifting, uncertain milieu like that described by this influential text. His theme is the perilous connection between wealth and social change.

In *The Liberal Imagination* (1951), Lionel Trilling wrote that a certain kind of hero reappeared in nineteenth-century novels, the Young Man from the

Provinces. This figure, who starts out with neither money nor status, creates a new identity by forcing entry into the upper classes. The last such figure, Trilling wrote, was Jay Gatsby.[9] The idea may have wider applications: Daisy Fay is possibly no more than herself, but if Gatsby is a version of Eugène de Rastignac then she is inescapably a version of Delphine de Nucingen. Her character expands considerably when that is considered. Daisy has more on her mind than the invidious difference between old and new money. She has been placed in Louisville for a reason. While Chicago was known for the kind of wealth Tom Buchanan represents, Louisville, as described by local historians, was a place of "huge factories" that "arose from the spirit of our local citizens." They operated at high risk so that fear was a very considerable economic motive. Daisy's house is overwhelming because of its appearance and also because it represents faith (with fingers crossed) that profitable enterprise would "last for generations." That house incarnates the obligation to succeed.[10] A life devoted to such values and anxieties had a heavy weight to bear. It might well be uncertain and inconstant. The central fact is that the rich in Fitzgerald do not have unlimited power—which makes them not less but more equivocal.

Even after *The Great Gatsby*, when class began to fade as a distinction, Fitzgerald continued to provide an audience of wage earners with different kinds of narratives of wealth. Scott Donaldson describes relative income in Fitzgerald, which reflects the facts of daily life.[11] The literary facts are also important. Fitzgerald got from novels by Austen, Balzac, Dickens, and James a sense of rentier capitalism's broad social effects, chief among them the power exerted by wealth over those without it. *Tender Is the Night* comes first to mind, although stories taking place from 1910 to 1920 also develop the subject. The Josephine stories, for example, are culturally jittery, filled with allusions to wealth and moral uncertainty. The Basil stories, which take place a few years before them, have an entirely different understanding of the problems of money and a much steadier tone. The Josephine stories take place under a new kind of public scrutiny. The reader is always conscious of the pressure exerted by the outside world on the family world.

Piketty identifies three groups (in the economy of the West and also in literature) competing for wealth before 1920. The top centile both in life and art was comprised of those with unearned incomes. However—and this is what confirms Fitzgerald's accuracy—there was additionally a managerial class that attained "top capital incomes" and a "patrimonial middle class" with its own share of national wealth. The latter are certainly in Fitzgerald's fiction.

In the Basil stories, which begin before 1914, there is a sense of equilibrium. That is not because the war is some years off. Times have been peaceful and, more important, stable. The Panic of 1907 was over, and there were not yet high income taxes or inflation. After 1914, when the Josephine stories begin, the atmosphere changes. Her stories are full of *social* hostility. The war contributes to that, as does life in a large city with its competing interests. So does a world in which new taxes "on dividends, interest, profits, and rents" affect life radically.[12] As the sequence proceeds, more issues attach themselves to what began simply as a story of wealth.

Assets became news and conspicuous consumption was covered by the press. However, there were many opinions on the use of riches from 1910 to 1920. The Progressive movement bequeathed to Fitzgerald and other writers its own sense of violent social disproportion: "Why should the lavish life-style of the upper ten matter to us? . . . the apparent trivialities of balls and parties counted for a great deal in turn-of-the-century America. The culture of the upper ten—half perversion and half repudiation of Victorianism—made their wealth and power all the more controversial. Elite values would repel the middle class enough to turn respectable Victorians into radicals."[13] Yet the stupendous selfishness of the upper classes attracted readers. As difficult as it was for the Progressives to comprehend, consumers wanted to imitate ownership. Everyone understood that yachts, castles, and art collections were too expensive for most people to own. But they could be copied in the elided form of boats, bungalows, and reproductions.[14] In *The Great Gatsby*, Myrtle Wilson, who is working class, lives amid images of Versailles. She uses the language of the upper class as that had been imagined by movies and magazines.

Wealth is a public topic. Even deep in the provinces, the benighted Mr. Gatz has heard about millionaires who "helped build up the country."[15] John T. Ungar, another provincial, can say, "I like very rich people. The richer a fella is, the better I like him."[16] He is crude but not odd. According to H. L. Mencken in the *Smart Set*, 1920, the "reputation" of wealth might be our most important asset under a democracy valuing "money far beyond its worth." Mencken often wrote in the form of small narratives that were developed by his disciples. Here is one we recognize in Fitzgerald: "the man who is thought to be poor never gets a fair chance. No one wants to listen to him. No one gives a damn what he thinks or knows or feels. No one has any desire for his good opinion." On the other hand, having money makes "one's political hallucinations worthy of attention."[17] We think of Gordon Sterrett in "May Day," who is effectively silenced by the power of money, and then of Tom

Buchanan, who is empowered by it in *The Great Gatsby*. In 1925, Keynes wrote that wealth was far too crudely conceived by moralists. He thought that the "social approbation of money" was more culturally important than possession or expenditure.[18] In short, it was not the possession of wealth that mattered so much as its cultural effects. Piketty's *Capital* describes what he sees on American video—the portrayal of "decadent young heirs and heiresses with little merit or virtue living shamelessly on family money."[19] That is a splendid review of the northwestern part of Los Angeles County as seen from the Left Bank, but more is involved than expenditure. Piketty understands that there is a pornography of wealth—and an intellectual subindustry apologizing for it. In "The Diamond as Big as the Ritz" the pleasures of mindless acquisition mean infinitely less than the ideas defending it.

According to Mencken, wealth was normalized by "society columns in the newspapers."[20] Resettlement from provinces to cities created a new kind of reader. There really is no more yellow journalism, nor does there need to be: "in its place are the harmless tabloids. They ease his envy by giving him a vicarious share in the debaucheries of his economic superiors. He is himself, of course, unable to roar about the country in a high-powered car . . . but when he reads of the scions of old Knickerbocker families doing it he somehow gets a touch of the thrill. It flatters him to think that he lives in a community in which such levantine joys are rife. Thus his envy is obscured by civic pride, by connoisseurship, and by a simple animal delight in good shows."[21] According to Walter Lippmann, there was a subindustry of praise for men "who in the magazines devoted to the religion of success appear as Makers of America."[22] Evidently, some men looked like malefactors of great wealth, some looked like benefactors of great wealth, and some looked like mediocrities of great wealth. All were subjects of public opinion and of Fitzgerald's fiction.

❋

Fitzgerald had to bring the nineteenth-century novel of money up to date. The attitudes of the Warren family in *Tender Is the Night* have to be made intelligible because their story needs daily motivation apart from its original sin. The opinions of Tom Buchanan in *The Great Gatsby* have to be understood so they have to be traced. The social power of the Perry family in the Josephine stories was best handled, Fitzgerald decided, by dialogue about the choices its members made. In general, the pursuit of fortune in the old novel gives way to the pursuit of ideas.

Fitzgerald sets his scenes in historically accurate detail. The Basil stories are dimly aware that in or around December 1910, human character changed. The Josephine stories, which begin in 1914, are more informed about that. Philipp Blom's *The Vertigo Years* asks a central question: what did the monied and literate classes have on their minds? Cues about change were in unexpected places: "Not for them the confident naturalism of Thomas Hardy, Theodor Fontane and Gustave Flaubert. . . . Their view of things was shaped by reading about races in fast machines and in children's magazines, by overhearing adult whispers about nervous breakdowns and fast women, by a daily life increasingly dominated by cities, newspapers and an intense relation to the future . . . an age had ended and a new one . . . was bursting onto the scene, visible as yet only in flashes and fragmented visions. Their work was jagged, shot through with undigested rushes of information, pushing their way into art as noise, collage, or quotation; by splintered faces, swirling shapes and imploded personalities."[23]

Fitzgerald recognized that a "view of things" was socially embodied by patronage and style. In "A Snobbish Story," civic institutions demand support and provide respectability. The Perrys have "stood behind the opera here for many years" (264), and Josephine's father is persuaded to bankroll a Little Theatre production. The ladies of Lake Forest support a vaudeville show featuring Travis de Coppet in a white satin football suit—Josephine likes the idea although that might be casting Fred Astaire as Douglas Fairbanks. She has a tryst in "First Blood" with Anthony Harker at the "Philanthrophilogical Building" in Grant Park, which is probably the Art Institute of Chicago. Supporting social class is tricky because civic institutions market conceptions as well as arts and letters. In the spring of 1914, when the Josephine stories begin, the respectable classes were being told by the Art Institute of Chicago that a new wave of artists had cut their ties (and evidently our own) to "the tranquil ideals of William Morris." These artists were "strongly influenced by all the latest French liberators, from Cézanne to Picasso." The actual subject was personal liberation, and the catalog flattered a patron's self-esteem. A connection was posited between art and audience. Current artists, both men and women, will soon "terrify the conservatives" everywhere and "are already setting Paris by the ears."[24] There are broad hints about sexual arrangements among artists and explicit reminders to the audience that Victorianism is obsolete. The catalog states that we can appeal only to the future; Blom states that there is an "intense relation" between personality and the future; Fitzgerald states that Josephine represents the future "in her own person."[25] But, the Art Institute of Chicago is more than happy to use culture as a commodity.[26]

As Blom points out, change causes anxiety. Josephine is tuned to the moment, and her narrative is insistent, jagged, keyed to anxiety. The Basil stories are sonorous; a typical pattern of language in "The Captured Shadow" will slowly reconsider ideas and states of mind. Basil's life is summarized by the labored conjugation of *connaître*, a Cartesian pun by a writer who knew philosophy. Josephine lives in the moment, internalizing opposites abruptly. "A Snobbish Story" has her "impatient for a change" (245), contradicting herself once or twice per page. Even the narrator has trouble; the story begins by stating that "it is difficult" to live down the past and goes through a tortuous sequence of "because," "but," and "certainly" that modifies the phrases that follow and also our sense of what may be actual.

The mention of historical time in the story implies relativity. It is mid-1916 and the Battle of the Somme has started, "but the war had become second-page news" (245). Against this large event dimly understood is a tennis match in Lake Forest. Outside the story, there are now even more directives from the Art Institute of Chicago about living "unrestrained" lives based on the "liberty of the individual to express himself in his own way."[27] New artists matter because *their* style transfers itself to *our* lives. Like Josephine, they are described as the newest thing. This kind of news about being new, Santayana wrote, has a "*public* force" that "lies entirely in the social blast that carried it, with magic conviction, into many minds at once."[28]

There is evidence for that. Josephine's letters to Anthony Harker in "First Blood" (1914) had "inevitably much quoting of lines from current popular songs, as if they expressed the writer's state of mind more fully than verbal struggles of her own" (198). Ruth Prigozy has noted that one Fitzgerald flapper became the "literary equivalent of Clara Bow: her lack of education, her bouncy charm, and her sexually charged behavior" were transferable.[29] "Among the top tunes of 1914 are Clarice Mayne's "I Was a Good Little Girl 'till I Met You" and "If I Had My Way" by the Peerless Quartet. "A Snobbish Story" has its own matrix. "Chin-Chin" ran on Broadway for nearly all of 1915, offering exactly the kind of sentimentalized love ("Let me see your pretty face, dear / All I want is one embrace, dear") that Josephine describes in her letters but does not exist in real life.[30] In 1916 there are flattering self-conceptions in Al Jolson's "You're a Dangerous Girl" and "Naughty! Naughty! Naughty!" by Joe Goodwin and William Tracey. In fact, John Bailey tells Josephine what he thinks of her through the language of lyrics:

"Listen, How would you like to be in this play?"

"Oh, I couldn't—I've got to be in a play out at the Lake."

"Society stuff," he said, scornfully mimicking: "Here come the jolly, jolly golfing girls. Maybe they'll sing us a song."

(256)

Josephine is conscious of harmonies and at the tournament sings along to a popular lyric. It describes love and the self very much as Bailey implies, melodious innocence untouched by reality (249). As social classes intersect, sound in this story changes from assonance to dissonance. At the workshop, Josephine registers "a flow of talk, rapt of expression but only half-comprehending" (254). Later, there is "uninfectious laughter" dying away (255) and rage beneath the ordinary rhythms of speech. Not all of it is caused by Josephine threatening to join the show; it is simply a fact of working lives.

By then, black music was not only in Chicago but also on Broadway. It would have been difficult to avoid W. H. Handy's "Memphis Blues" of 1912 or "St. Louis Blues" of 1914. Bert Williams was by 1914 a major figure in the Ziegfeld Follies; Spencer Williams did "I Ain't Got Nobody" in 1916. Fitzgerald reminds us at length in *The Great Gatsby* that "Beale Street Blues" of 1916 forcibly affected Daisy's sense of self. Just after the war in "The Offshore Pirate" Ardita and Curtis listen to "the low sound of singing" by a black band and literally find their own identities.[31] A certain part of Josephine's identity has been prefigured by music and lyrics about passion, loss, and suffering. She does sing the blues a lot.

Josephine and John Bailey have ideas on their mind that are essentially public opinions. Some of them were covered by Josiah Royce's *The Nature and the Need of Loyalty* (1908), an apology for the past and a bon voyage to the coming decade: "We have become accustomed, during the past few generations—during the period of Socialism and of Individualism, of Karl Marx, of Henry George, of Ibsen, of Nietzsche, of Tolstoi—to hear unquestionably sincere lovers of humanity sometimes declaring our traditions regarding the rights of property to be immoral, and sometimes assailing, in the name of virtue, our present family ties. . . . Individualism itself . . . speaks in the name of the true morality of the future."[32] Two of Royce's points are in Fitzgerald: the first, that American problems might be caused by family, class, and money; the second, that "our moral standards themselves are questioned."[33]

Not all those beliefs listed by Royce have survived history, but Henry George and Individualism once thrived in American minds. They provide at least

some of the ammunition for Josephine's antagonist John Boynton Bailey—
who is himself a Young Man from the Provinces. Bailey is in the story for a
number of reasons and first among them is his excellence as a character. But
he is also there because he is a very quirky individualist, embodying in his own
personality (and his relationship with Josephine) a major issue of the moment.
Just as Royce was listing Individualism among other challenges to things as
they were, Georg Simmel produced his well-known argument that civilization
had to make a choice between incorporating individual freedom and character into the social system—or simply allowing it to devolve into a thousand
idiosyncrasies. Simmel was especially concerned with the way that life in the
metropolis allowed character to find solace not in action but in retreat from
action: within an inert and monied life.[34] Even more important was the work of
William James, who gave the subject its American habitation and a name. Well
before 1910, James had published his opinion that "the individual, the person
in the singular number, is the more fundamental phenomenon, and the social
institution, of whatever grade, is but secondary and ministerial."[35] That idea is
at the center of the intellectual chaos of Fitzgerald's story. The problem is not
the truth of James's statement but the map for getting there.

Eight scenes are set in "A Snobbish Story," beginning with the grandstand
at Lake Forest. After that, lunch at the old La Grange Hotel, a taxi, a theater
workshop, another taxi on Lake Shore Drive, a movie, the Perry home, then
back to the tennis tournament where no one wants to think about the Battle of
the Somme. The first encounter of Josephine and John Bailey becomes almost
formally dialectical:

> "I never saw you before."
> "I never saw you either, but you looked so nice in your hat, and I saw
> you smiling to your friends, so I thought I'd take a chance."
> "Like you do downstate, hey, Cy?" retorted Josephine insolently.
> "What's the matter with downstate? I come from Abe Lincoln's town,
> where the boys are big and brilliant."
> (248)

The things that matter are their attraction to each other—and also what is on
their mind. Almost immediately they begin to argue about issues identified by
Royce as the main conflicts of the new decade: class, money, and individualism.

Josephine goes to lunch with Bailey the next day at the old La Grange and
sees her father with a peroxide blonde. She draws the wrong inference, leaves

the scene, but finds that her next stop won't put her mind at ease. Bailey takes her to a crowded theater workshop, where she suddenly understands that "everybody there, except herself, was crazy" (254). She isn't being dismissive. The narrator states that she "was for the moment right" and theater history indicates why. The people she meets want major parts in real productions. They don't use manners to hide fear, jealousy, and rage. And they understand that doing a play in Lake Forest—"She thinks it's a dramatic club, like Miss Pinkerton's school" (255)—makes pleasant imaginings. The world as it is resists order, and their part of it shows the lonely crowd comprised of "strangers to each other."[36] They have already been part of communities that don't work.

Josephine reacts to ideas indirectly. The narrator takes pains to tell the reader how scenes register on Josephine's mind. Her opinions aren't so much declared as described. Until now, Josephine's expectations have been founded on the logic of social order. Her family represents the community, and in a fairly exalted way. But there are new ideas about association. For example, there are all those souls, in "Chicago, in 1916—ignorant, wild with energy, doggedly sensitive and helplessly romantic, wanderers like their prairie ancestors upon the face of the land" (254). It will be impossible in this story as in political reality to fit them all into one social structure. The language of description implies that because Fitzgerald describes Chicago as Eliot describes London: "pervading everything a terribly strange, brooding mystery of rooftops and empty apartments, of white dresses in the paths of parks, and fingers for stars and faces instead of moons, and people with strange people scarcely knowing one another's names" (257). Fitzgerald emphasizes numbers, strangeness, anonymity—all subjects that have until now had no connection to Josephine's mind. Those subjects clearly have a common source, and even a common language.

The story has been about writing from the beginning—although not about how much better Carl Sandburg is than Shakespeare. The passage is about the way that metropolis is beginning to be symbolically understood. It echoes Eliot—who by 1930, the year of the story's composition, had become part of the public domain. As the narrator states, "Josephine's imagination rested here." In *Axel's Castle* (1931), at very much the same time, Edmund Wilson used the same language for cityscape, writing about its sense of "nameless millions" living incoherent lives. As he saw it, seeing metropolis in this way leads directly to doubts about American "institutions" and "bankrupt ideals."[37] That idea may be a blunt instrument—in Fitzgerald, human organization resists ordering because it resists knowing.

Writing in 1930 about stage, lyrics, and vaudeville, Fitzgerald describes a new industry. The aspiring cast of that Little Theatre play is itself divided intractably. "Artistic or economic ideals" (254) are not as real as needs. Hysteria and suspicion are industrial norms, as are "bitter hatred" and "impulsive demonstrations."[38] If these people are crazy, that is because of consequences rather than aberrations. You start early to get the job, so children leave school to find work; husbands and wives are impediments so other arrangements have to be made; alternatives to making it big are playing saloons and sleeping on sawdust floors. As George Burns said in an interview, "so that's the job we had—waking up drunks. Big future there."[39]

Fitzgerald's text keeps urging comparison with the world outside the story. Actors in that workshop will, he says, dominate American theater "for a decade" thereafter (254). Josephine is conscious of her own rebellion—but these men and women had already "undermined Victorianism."[40] Within a year of the Josephine stories Fitzgerald developed that subject in "Echoes of the Jazz Age" (1931). He writes that movies and fiction from Valentino to James Joyce described conditions already "familiar in our contemporary life." And that movies of the Jazz Age "had no effect upon its morals" because productions balked at reflecting actual experience.[41] The Josephine stories do a better job than popular music or movies explaining what is really happening in the social world:

> "It's very original," said Josephine breathlessly. "Which would I be?"
> "You'd be the girl the married man was in love with."
> "The white one?"
> "Sure, no miscegenation in this play."
> She would look up the word when she got home.
> "Is that the part that girl was going to play?"
> "Yes." He frowned, and then added, "She's my wife."
> "Oh—you're married?"
> "I married young—like the man in my play. In one way it isn't so bad, because neither of us believed in the old-fashioned bourgeois marriage, living in the same apartment and all. She kept her own name. But we got to hate each other anyhow."
> (256–57)

The essay and this story are part of Fitzgerald's sequence of reflections on depicting social life. They are also part of a series of questionings about America that included William James, John Dewey, and Walter Lippmann. Lippmann's 1927 essay on the fiction of Sinclair Lewis begins *before* 1920, at "the close of that period of democratic idealism and of optimism" when people thought life could by changed, even made perfect. By 1920, "the American people were thoroughly weary of their old faith. . . . They had found out that the problem of living is deeper and more complex than they had been accustomed to think it was." Conditions seemed ideal for good social novelists—but Lippmann did not think that Lewis was among them. He created stereotypes, not characters. Far more important, he never came close to discerning American complexity. Lippmann states his standards—which are effectively those of Fitzgerald. "Although we are all endowed with eyes, few of us see very well. We see what we are accustomed to see, and what we are told to see. To the rest of what is about us we are largely anesthetic, for we live in a kind of hazy dream bent on our purposes. For the apprehension of the external world, and of that larger environment that is invisible, we are almost helpless until we are supplied with patterns of seeing that enable us to fix objects clearly amid the illegible confusion of experience."[42]

There is a silent moment after John Bailey tells Josephine that she is beautiful and that he is a great writer—and also descended from Charlemagne. Josephine understands that what he says is only partially connected to what he means. He knows that when she says that she likes poetry she is really saying that she likes him. She knows that he is something definite and real, with a "particular and special passion for life" (252). That doesn't mean she is a good person, but it does mean that she sees how realities are buried in styles.

Josephine sees more than the prescribed social views of her family. She is more frank than the movies. There is a guide to her insight in a letter from Ginevra King to Fitzgerald in 1915: "the inner workings of my mind would or would not be of interest to you, as the case may be—But I do think a lot though, more than people think I do, although I haven't very much sense. I have more than some people credit me with I hope, only I don't know how to use it."[43] "A Snobbish Story" is not about Josephine being good or bad but about Fitzgerald being right or wrong about the way things are.

"Echoes of the Jazz Age" sounds a great deal like Lippmann because it goes back to the "complicated origins" of the 1920s. The essay itself begins with "the first social revelation. . . . As far back as 1915."[44] It deals in ambiguities (among them the choice of preserving righteousness or losing children). The Josephine stories constitute a long and very successful effort to show such social ambiguities. The stories account for a new historical context in which great wealth is not isolated—say, as it might be in a chateau located in the Rocky Mountains. Mr. Perry has some shape to him: "I'm not afraid of things simply because they're new" (264). He doesn't beg for today to be just like yesterday. Wealth has to deal with a modern world that is more interesting than its own. It will have ambiguous reactions. It is entirely possible that Josephine Perry as a character is an act of literary revenge—Fitzgerald did turn Ginevra King into Judy Jones in one of her incarnations. But the Josephine stories are a small *Comédie humaine,* packed with formidable characters who try to work out their own narratives of life in a social world ever less contained by money and class.

5

A NICE GIRL FROM LOUISVILLE

In March 1918, Lieutenant F. Scott Fitzgerald was stationed at Camp Zachary Taylor outside of Louisville, Kentucky; in June he was at Camp Sheridan near Montgomery, Alabama; and in October he served at Camp Mills on Long Island. There were other postings but these three became part of literary history. Impressions of each were incorporated into his stories and novels of the 1920s. Army life was not the only thing he transposed: Fitzgerald met Zelda in Montgomery and invented for Jordan Baker and Daisy Fay a social life drawn from Louisville. That life was *haute bourgeoisie* and did not imitate the plantocracy of the deep South. Daisy and Jordan are from the Appalachian South—Louisville is 270 miles from Chicago, much closer than that to Bloomington, Columbus, and Cincinnati.[1] It was never a backwater or lost place in history and remains one of the great exhibits of the Gilded Age. Old Louisville was useful to *The Great Gatsby* because of what he saw—and also because the city so notably practiced the religion of success.

Fitzgerald's account of army life in his letters matches archives of the Camp Zachary Taylor Historical Society. Camp Taylor was the largest recruit camp in the United States, constituting a world of its own. It brought together huge numbers of men who rapidly found themselves wishing they were somewhere else. It looked nothing like West Point or other places with long historical traditions. Camp Taylor was built quickly, wood on flat ground that turned to mud. We tend to think that the shape and style of New York City affected the Jazz Age but so did the experience of mass life at military training camps. Fitzgerald's close friends Edmund Wilson and John Peale Bishop also served in the war and recognized this effect. Their correspondence with Fitzgerald is about their own existential pointlessness. Lewis Dabney, Wilson's biographer, says that Wilson spread two ideas about service to his friends and his audience. First was the rage of living a life without form: "submerged in the 'profanity, obscenity, and pure stupidity' of the army, no longer in rational control of his life." Second was the discovery of new "habits and standards" of social life. It was, Dabney writes, disconcerting but also "liberating" to find another social world.[2]

Life at Camp Taylor was at the lower end of liberation. Letters on file at the Camp Zachary Taylor Historical Society describe the material facts of life in 1917–18: endless drills, lessons on saluting, Kitchen Police for enlisted men, study of manuals by officers as well as other ranks, days spent hauling equipment that no one needed, dealing with those who were even worse at marching, digging, and leading troops than the self-absorbed Lieutenant F. Scott Fitzgerald. Soldiers at Camp Taylor expected hardship but not the endless irrationality of being trained in one specialty, then assigned to another; marching back and forth not only for drills but also as punishment; and being exiled from an understood social world. Wilson wrote to Fitzgerald that he had become "sterilized, suppressed, and blighted" by life at Base Hospital 36 near Detroit; he wrote to Stanley Dell that he spent most of his week "cursing the results of American civilization."[3] John Peale Bishop, also in the infantry, wrote to Fitzgerald about missing beauty, books, talk, women, coffee, and especially romance. Fitzgerald wrote to his cousin Sally that he missed such things—and even the boredom of Saint Paul.[4] As for romance, Fitzgerald found it in the unexpected form of place shaped by money: "He went to her house, at first with other officers from Camp Taylor, then alone. It amazed him—he had never been in such a beautiful house before. But what gave it an air of breathless intensity was that Daisy lived there—it was as casual a thing to her as his tent out at camp was to him. There was a ripe mystery about it, a hint of bedrooms upstairs more beautiful and cool than other bedrooms, of gay and radiant activities taking place through its corridors and of romances that were not musty and laid away already in lavender but fresh and breathing and redolent of this year's shining motor cars and of dances whose flowers were scarcely withered."[5] Robert Beuka has mentioned "a changing and often alienating landscape" in Fitzgerald.[6] The chaos of Camp Taylor—mass life in muddy fields—had to be crossed before getting to this place. Daisy's house is not self-defining but part of a landscape—and an economy.

The scene implies stability over generations. Yet the city containing it was industrial; Louisville's money came from sales and production. Uncertainty about life was built in. The city was not a branch of national corporate industry; much of its money was home grown. Its entrepreneurs owned tractor factories, furniture warehouses, and metal-working plants that they had founded. These were subject to risk. The religion of success is not a metaphor; if there was a Genesis that told of investment, growth, and profit there was also an Apocalypse of bankruptcy, loss of customers, and failure. In the old business style, entrepreneurs wanted to control manufacturing from raw materials to machined forms. That increases costs. They could not rely on corporate help for shortfalls because that was the price of independence. So their domestic style translated something of their anxiety. It showed success through acquisition, using the most permanent of materials.[7] The effect of permanence implied freedom from necessity.

Servicing the wealthy was an industry in itself. The town was known for its commercial buildings and for one building in particular, the Seelbach Hotel, which to this day insists that Fitzgerald began *The Great Gatsby* by writing drafts of the novel on cocktail napkins at the bar. It retails the wedding of Tom and Daisy Buchanan, encouraging customers to imitate that event at the Grand Ballroom. Louisville wasn't a shy place: "Immediately after dusk the city became a veritable dreamland of dazzling brilliancy when the electric current was turned on a hundred designs and decorative structures. The entire central portion of the city is tonight flooded with light from myriads of vari-colored incandescent globes. Great Templar crosses and shields adorn the entire fronts of office buildings and business houses. Crusaders and prancing war horses of heroic design constructed of cathedral glass behind which are placed electric lights are conspicuous figures on some of the public buildings. Festoons of colored light span the thoroughfares of forty different blocks in the heart of the city." That describes a gala week for a civic organization in 1901, reported with some envy by visitors from another state.[8] Those four private railroad cars and the string of pearls from Chicago fitted right in.

Louisville was a river town, a racetrack town, and a home to army encampments from the Civil War on. The facts of life included saloons, crowds of good-timers, gambling, and a flourishing branch of the world's oldest profession. When the chairman of the federal commission on training camps ordered that Louisville's red-light district be closed in 1917 in order to protect Camp Taylor, the mayor refused on the grounds that he did not want ladies to be evicted from their homes. For most of the twentieth century Louisville was behind only New York, San Francisco, Seattle, and Washington, DC, in its rate of prostitution.[9] That says something about values, but more about enterprise.

There were two Louisvilles. Of course barriers existed between territories but they were just personal. Fitzgerald thought that W. C. Handy had provided Daisy with an alternative identity in "Beale Street Blues"—which appeared in 1916. Even earlier, by 1914, the upper class defined itself through standards of sophistication rather than those of domesticity. As current scholarship states, the war came *after* social changes, not before.[10]

Midwestern Victorian style is unlike New England or San Francisco. The houses on Summit Avenue in Saint Paul and Third Street in Louisville are economic trophies. In Louisville, exteriors are ornamented with stonework columns, balustrades, and porticos. Interiors are majestic although heavy on the eye. Even the bedrooms intuited by Fitzgerald can be seen because many photographs have been taken over the years by design, landscape, and architectural magazines.[11] To judge from photographic evidence, the emphasis was on handworked elements: wood, plaster, tile, stone. It would not be possible today to duplicate the woods used, especially in the Conrad-Caldwell House Museum or the Ferguson, Mengel, and Dodd buildings. They were old growth, exotic, built at a time when woodwork was a local art as well as industry.

Interiors have intricate and rather astonishing parquet inlay, coffered ceilings, carved mantels, and paneling. These houses are not intended to be comfortable, at least not as a first priority: wall space is used for decoration rather than opened up to light, while furniture is essentially an object to be carved, painted, and ornamented. The total effect is that of money on display.[12] That is borne out by the division of these places into public and private spaces, with separate rooms, really barriers, for visitors. A reconsideration of Edith Wharton's *The Decoration of Houses* (1897) emphasizes that turn-of-the-century design meant cultural conflict. Victorianism showed acquisition; the new style showed utility. Vast social differences were implied by "exterior and interior and the décor of a room."[13] Fitzgerald describes the amplitude of floors, rooms, and corridors, implying the distance between social classes. We can see that even the backstage of social life was complex: there were design wars between display and the older virtue of restraint, and the constant object (specified in Fitzgerald's Josephine stories about Chicago) of maintaining style appropriate to degree of wealth. Simply to look at one of the great bourgeois homes was to recognize ideas in the form of styles. And yet, from the inside of the house things looked different. In order to sustain social life there had to be a flow of cash unimpeded by debt, obligation, or the limits of credit. Social standards—and also appearances—had to be kept up. Anyone living on Third Street might have had these things in mind.

※

Both Jordan and Gatsby describe Daisy in Louisville. Where Gatsby is lyrical, Jordan is mathematical. Her passage is one of the most quantified in Fitzgerald: "the largest of the banners and the largest of the lawns belonged to Daisy Fay's house. She was just eighteen, two years older than me, and by far the most popular of all the young girls in Louisville. She dressed in white and had a little white roadster and all day long the telephone rang in her house and excited young officers from Camp Taylor demanded the privilege of monopolizing her that night, 'anyways for an hour!'" (59). There are ten allusions to quantity in three sentences. Even larger numbers are implied since any comparison is relative: if Daisy's house is the largest then there are undisclosed numbers of other houses in the background. In the account book of her mind those ten references to measurement become a universe perceived through time, size, and place. The "most popular," "all the young girls," and "all day long" have a cumulative effect greater than any numbers denoted. The language Fitzgerald gives her implies that Jordan sees everything as one prolonged calculation. That is clearly part of her personality—but there are cultural reasons for the way she thinks. She seems imbued with Louisville's businesslike mores. *Middletown*, for example, calls midwestern industrial life "instrumental" because the economy dominates the community. Specifically, *Middletown* defines the choices we make as consequences of the money available for them. It had become plain that a life "inherently satisfying" would not, given the limits of income, be a life chosen.[14]

Jordan describes Daisy before the wedding with that string of pearls from Tom worth "three hundred and fifty thousand dollars." It's mentioned more than once—but all we know is how much it costs. What it looks like doesn't matter to Jordan; what it represents matters greatly to Daisy. Who, when we see her with those pearls, is drunk but conscious: "she groped around in a waste-basket she had with her on the bed and pulled out the string of pearls. 'Take 'em downstairs and give 'em back to whoever they belong to'" (60–61). But after that, keeping silence, she also becomes an object of great value to whoever she belongs to. And yet, far more has gone into her own calculation than first appears. Alex Danchev's biography of Cézanne has a considerable passage about implication, citing a critic who watched him working in 1906. He was "perhaps the most precise and realistic of contemporary painters. The intermittent romanticism of his style is a splendid garment he uses to dress up the nakedness of his impressions. He makes use of very simple notations."[15]

What matters is the result of such notation: "the amount of truth" that can be drawn out of a represented object has its limits. Character can't be fully accounted for until shown through its responses. Cézanne's critic praised his delineation but concluded that the engagement of self with feeling was even more important. Character was as much enactment as depiction. But there is another dimension because character is to some extent culturally determined.

Daisy was the first "nice" girl Gatsby had ever known. The term is a long way off now, but it meant something before the 1920s—and it was on Fitzgerald's mind for a number of years. Edmund Wilson was eager to do a book about army life and wrote to Fitzgerald about it in 1919: "Stan Dell and I have conceived a literary project in which you might possibly help us. Our idea is to write a new *Soirées de Médan* on the American part in the war. The original *Soirées de Médan* was a set of short stories published after the Franco-Prussian War by a group of realistic writers headed by Zola . . . and I have written to John Bishop and a number of others. . . . One of the remarkable virtues of the *Soirées* was the fact that they dealt not only with the front but also with the mismanagement of the war by the government, the effect on the civilian population, and the stagnation of the troops behind the lines . . . let us have something about army life in the States during the war."[16] Wilson told Dell some of his thoughts about meeting girls while at Base Hospital 36 outside of Detroit. He was in a part of the Midwest "where the daughters know apparently literally nothing about anything except the pleasant, the gentle, and the nice. They are so pretty, so fine, and so ill educated; they know that woman's place is in the home and have no other desire or aim except to exhibit the domestic virtues. The age, the nation has passed them by; they are little girls at twenty."[17] Wilson and Fitzgerald look at the same thing but see it differently. Wilson may have been right about women of the upper middle class, but only if ideas determine selves. Fitzgerald wrote about other forms of perception. Sally Carol Happer in "The Ice Palace" uses the term "energy" to describe her motivation. The term she uses comes from William James who thought that no one could make reasonable decisions without vitality or the power to enforce them. In "The Offshore Pirate," Ardita Farnum chooses "what you like always" over "other people's opinions."[18] She is reading *The Revolt of the Angels* by Anatole France, which begins with a warning about opinion: "in the century in which we live there are so many modes of belief that future historians will have difficulty in finding their way about."[19] She throws it at her guardian—who may be standing in for all other arbiters of mind like Edmund Wilson. Fitzgerald later placed this novel on a list of indispensable books. These two stories replicate a pattern in his fiction: moral and intellectual certainties are confronted by contradiction. The result is a dialogue of relativity.

A number of things happened between 1917 when Wilson recorded his impression of Detroit's middle class and the early 1920s. In 1918, Mencken published *In Defense of Women* with this notice: men "have forced upon women an artificial character which well conceals their real character, and women have found it profitable to encourage the deception."[20] Mencken added many other essays to the national dialogue about woman, not all of them convincing. But he recognized that women could be intelligent without being educated, and he informed his audience how they functioned in that most dishonest of arrangements, "the present organization of society."[21] He was relentless in his correction of social myopia. He understood that there had been huge social changes before America's entry into the war, stating in 1916 that "the veriest school-girl of today knows as much as the midwife of 1885."[22]

In the light of his reading and experience, Fitzgerald thought about his original assignment—and then created instead an affair at an army base. *The Beautiful and Damned* is about nice girls, girls who want to be nice, and bad girls down on their luck doing business on Jackson Street. John Peale Bishop had warned Fitzgerald to avoid sociology in the novel.[23] According to Bishop, the novel should be about feeling and experience, not banal social facts. Yet Fitzgerald thought it important to set Dot Raycroft against a background of social probabilities. "Had she been born to a higher stratum," she might have escaped the common experience of women on the fringes of war. Wilson, who edited this novel, recognized his own advice about setting character within social conditions. He can't have been pleased by Fitzgerald's apolitical concentration on the facts of life: "Dorothy Raycroft was nineteen. Her father had kept a small, unprosperous corner store, and she had graduated from high school in the lowest fourth of her class two days before he died. At high school she had enjoyed a rather unsavory reputation. . . . As a rule things happened to Dot. She was not weak because there was nothing in her to tell her she was being weak. She was not strong, because she never knew that some of the things she did were brave. She neither defied nor conformed nor compromised."[24] This is unseen America. Lower-class hopes were not supported by middle-class conceptions. They were not even understood by the middle-class mind. It was essential that Fitzgerald work with naturalism in this novel because ideas were *obstacles*. "Working men, women, and children lived by a different set of cultural rules that also challenged Victorianism and aroused both fear and sympathy in the middle class."[25] That is a cut-and-dried state-ment by a historian of the Progressive movement, but we might add to it the kind of insight brought to the novel by Thomas Piketty's *Capital*. Their condi-tion was a natural subject for the novel because nothing else could remotely give the same sense of their diminished lives. Or of the distance between classes. Gatsby tells Nick that Daisy was his first "nice girl"—and also that "he had come in contact with such people but always with indiscernible barbed wire between" (116).

Dot Raycroft moves along from man to man, keeping her imaginative integrity; everything else she loses. She is much more interesting than Wil-son's idea of a nice girl—and hers is one of the first-rate love stories we have about the Great War. Fitzgerald has captured the experience of a country with many wars. More important, though, is his depiction of an unwilled life. He returned to the subject of "original" lives and their aftermath in *The Great Gatsby*. There were reasons to begin the story of Daisy Buchanan with that of Daisy Fay. Louisville is a mental point of origin for *The Great Gatsby*: the city had not only a social but also a literary history.

Part of that literary history was recent, well known, and sentimental. The interminable series of novels about local aristocracy by Annie Fellows John-ston had already been used by Fitzgerald in "Bernice Bobs Her Hair." In his story, Johnston is the source for a credo of Victorian social faith: certain mys-terious womanly qualities assure love. As Bernice knows, these stories are in-tended to be models for her own life. And, as Marjorie knows, they are the wrong models.

The Johnston novels about upper-class life outside Louisville proceed from childhood to schooling to engagement. Girlhood figures like "The Little Colo-nel" (a role later played by Shirley Temple) have the good sense to admire val-ues more than they do money, although they don't recognize that such choices can only be made by the privileged. The stories apply themes of romance to daily life. Johnston's *The Little Colonel at Boarding-School* (1903) describes ex-perience as a teenage girl might see it—or a writer selling the romantic South might see it for her:

> "What does that make you think of?" he asked.
> "Of a lovely September afternoon just like this," answered Betty, dreamily, half-closing her eyes and drawing in the fragrance with a slow, deep breath. "Of long shadows on the lawn and the sunshine flickering

through the locust leaves like gold, just as it is doing now. Of Malcolm MacIntyre sitting over where you are, thrumming on his banjo, and of Keith and you and Lloyd and me all singing 'My Old Kentucky Home.' Is that what it makes you think of?"

Servants (including a "faithful old nurse") are in the background.[26] In short, it is a posed portrait of culture as we would like to experience it, with the child-individual at the center of the universe. Freud read this kind of literature and wrote that fantasies of art induce a mild narcosis in viewers—although that never lasts long enough to confront the problems of actual social life.[27] Yet he was sympathetic to romances of daily life because they rethink what cannot be changed.

Bernice is for a time a believer in such stories, which is to say in the ideology of late Victorian culture. The narrative has implications because it is part of a series: after *The Little Colonel at Boarding-School* there was *The Little Colonel's Knight Comes Riding* (1907). Johnston kept on writing about men who were knightly and girls who get to marry them.[28] Assumptions about place, character, and style that come from texts enter social life: "The power of a sentimental novel to move its audience depends upon the audience's being in possession of the conceptual categories that constitute character and event. That storehouse of assumptions includes attitudes towards the family and toward social institutions; a definition of power and its relation to individual human feeling; notions of political and social equality; and above all a set of religious beliefs that organizes and sustains the rest."[29]

Tom tells Nick that Jordan is "a nice girl" (18) from Louisville, which seems simple enough; although we know from *The Beautiful and Damned* how evasive the phrase can be. Tom himself is consummately evasive. He avoids the hard edges of personal truth in his oration on family, friends, and community. Whatever he says is general because he grants immunity to individuals like himself. We begin to understand his investment in ambiguity; Jordan is "a nice girl" only because of her status. But there is a great deal more to his dialogue because it crosses contested literary terrain. Throughout the decade, Edmund Wilson depicted character as it originated in some community, then became changed by ideas. *I Thought of Daisy* and *The Higher Jazz*, novels about the 1920s, are aware of Fitzgerald's work and openly based on it. The differences between the two writers were not technical, although discussion seems to rest there.[30] Wilson's first novel of the 1920s has a heroine from the provinces who is evidently the true "Daisy"; while his second novel shows the socially impossible Ratsbys converted to imaginary "bootleggers."[31] Chekhov once remarked that having more poets than we need is culturally ominous.

Wilson hoped to prove that the old and new America could be (politically) reconciled and that character is changed by social belief. These ideas go against the grain of novels that shaped Fitzgerald's mind. They are an impossibility for Balzac. Wilson's own novels invoke the end of ideas "derived from our social class."[32] He understood the issue: In I Thought of Daisy, Rita (Edna St. Vincent Millay) is unable to forget "that life of the small American town, which she put on when she woke every morning, like some cursed indestructible dress of girlhood, too worn, too soiled, too small."[33] Daisy, who is far more symbolic than Fitzgerald's figure, takes the curse off life in Pittsburgh. She becomes an enactment "of the fluidity of manners in America, the plasticity of social position—of the swiftness and adventitiousness of the way in which such things changed."[34] Fitzgerald added an enormous historical parenthesis to the myth of social change. His southern women—Jordan, Daisy, Dot Raycroft, Ailie Calhoun—are always described in the impossible process of changing themselves because they can't change reality. I've mentioned that the dimension of place in Fitzgerald is always affected by the dimension of time; each of these characters tries to adjust to the social moment but is never really free of her original self. Even worse, the changes they make in order to become more popular, more marriageable, more at peace with their condition, don't work.

The early reviewers of The Great Gatsby were nervously consistent about its being "modern to the hour." They interpreted that as concentration on the immediate present, so we find continual references to the actual, the age, the current, the moment, and the times.[35] The text, however, refers to a landscape of the past.[36] Just as reviewers concluded that The Great Gatsby was a commentary on the present, John Dewey was writing that the present was an extension of the past. He wrote in 1927 that conceptions about America were useless without starting "from a community as a fact." Society was a consequence, he said, of early associations.[37] The Great Gatsby takes place in the summer of 1922 but is built around recollections of 1910–20. Like all acts of memory, they have been reconfigured. In 1921, just before the story is renewed, Bertrand Russell had written an account of memory in The Analysis of Mind. It wasn't by happenstance; from James and Bergson on, traditional philosophy had entered the realm of social philosophy. It became essential to evaluate the freedom of the modern mind—and, as a corollary, its dependence on the past. Russell was of course concerned with accuracy of perception of the past, but even more so with the weight of feeling we retain, hence the limits of human choice. Details of past life are guaranteed to elude us—but not the investment of feeling we have put into their recollection. He wrote, "in investigating memory-beliefs, there are certain points which must be borne in mind. In the first place, everything constituting a memory-belief is happening *now*, not in the past time to which the belief is said to refer."[38] So beliefs did not need to be true. They only needed to be convincing. That is a counterpart to Freud, arguing that, even in conscious thought, memory is a form of belief. The coldest and most detached Fitzgerald characters, Tom and Jordan, seem not to have any difficulty traversing the past. Nick and Daisy see the past as Russell describes it, in the form of experience that can't be forgotten. That is putting it in too neutral a way: it can't be escaped.

When Gatsby describes Daisy there is no mention of her being a southern belle. He tells Nick about her house, its furnishings, and its monied mystery. He recalls specifically the love that joins them, obstacles between them, and her character. Jordan recalls Daisy's house, wealth, and social standing. These are the longest accounts of Daisy in the novel and the only witnessed sources for her during the war. They are important for what they say and also for what they leave out. At no point is it implied that wealth has affected her character, although it is part of her condition. In fact, Gatsby—for a second time—sees "just how extraordinary a 'nice' girl could be."[39] In more ways than one: we recall for ourselves "the deep memory" both Gatsby and Daisy retain of their last afternoon in bed together. Given the work of Bergson, James, Russell, and Dewey, that phrase demands attention. The book is sometimes treated as a daydream of social class, but this is about something else. Daisy and Gatsby have a love affair and that—not the mythology of money—accounts for the depth of feeling in the story.

Gatsby may have an obsession, but it is not a fantasy.

Daisy describes herself in 1922, leaving out what Jordan and Gatsby have set down. She talks about innocence, youth, the passage of time, and her memory of southern girlhood. The moral independence of 1917 has been replaced. During the war Daisy has acted "herself"; after marriage she has a new persona. Part of the interest of the novel is her transformation from the generous and willful girl of 1917 to the formulaic wife of 1922. The persona she adopts has two sources, the first provided by conventional marriage. The

other is the most common form of parole from marriage, creation of a sentimental self absorbed by altruistic pleasures and duties. Sentimental novels
have the stated intention of preparing women for marriage and its aftermath.
Annie Fellows Johnston typically shows girls thinking about childhood innocence, wondering what time will bring, match-making for their friends, imagining poeticized landscapes that substitute for reality by deflecting attention
from the actual and necessary. Johnston heroines reflect on the circumstances
of friends, family, and even distant cousins. Innocence is often mentioned—it
is one of the great topics, with sexual, racial, and religious connotations. It is
connected to childhood and memory, allowing the female lead to see herself
free of the tangled obligations of social life. Few of these things are absent
from The Great Gatsby.

When Lionel Trilling wrote about this period of American life and literature—he was concentrating on Ethan Frome of 1911—he covered the idea of
morality rather than the very different idea of social inequality. Edith Wharton's novel had appeared at a time when Americans saw themselves in a way
unmatched by any other literature or time. They wanted innocence, and the
idea of morality meant submission to things as they were, not a heroic leap
into the dark. The qualities then admired were optimism, cheerfulness, and
gentility. Those qualities (Howells had called them the "smiling aspects of
life") did not mean the rejection of reality in the hope of discovering truth.
Passive acceptance or the morality of inertia defined the social self. Propriety
was a very great virtue. So while literature, as Trilling writes, is charmed by
energy it is also disarmed by stasis; it becomes difficult to think that Fitzgerald's Daisy Fay Buchanan has a moral life if she does not act against her
own inclination.[40] Freud thought that literary fantasy, the avoidance of moral
choice, was part of the middle-class mind. It rarely enabled readers to deal
with actuality—but he forgave it. This is what he said about the romances or
sentimental novels of that period: "if anyone is inclined to turn away in horror
from this depravity of the childish heart . . . he should observe that . . . none of
them really [is] so badly intended."[41]

Edmund Wilson concluded that nice girls said everything they knew but
les voix de silence were always there. Here is Georgia O'Keeffe in 1923, writing
about her Midwest: "I grew up pretty much as every[one] else grows up and
one day seven years ago found myself saying to myself—I can't live where I
want to—I can't go where I want to—I can't do what I want to—I can't even
say what I want to—School and things that painters have taught me even keep
me from painting as I want to. I decided I was a very stupid fool not to at least

paint as I wanted to—So these paintings and drawings happened and many others that are not here—I found that I could say things with color and shapes that I couldn't say in any other way—things that I had no words for."[42] Like Georgia O'Keeffe, Daisy has to say things indirectly. We can't recover a direct sense of Daisy's mind from reportage about her. Yet she changes more than critics concede. In 1917, she has the courage to love Gatsby, change her way of life, and oppose her parents when Gatsby leaves for the front. Between 1917 and 1922 she determines to conceal her personal life and to put up with Tom's serial infidelities. In the summer of 1922 she chooses to tell Nick about things that have happened and how she has yet again changed her mind. She goes back to Gatsby—and then betrays him. These are considerable decisions and her assumption of many roles indicates more than frailty. It would be superficial to say that these things are done purely reactively because Nick states that she had both "intentions" and "courage." Tom's explanation doesn't come close because the reason he gives for her leaving Gatsby—a "presumptuous little flirtation is over" (105)—is his idea of motivation, not hers. One of the great problems of the text is not the reason for her betrayal, but understanding her road to it.[43] When Nick ends the story, he remarks that he isn't "provincial" any more. That is to say the values he starts out with are ineffective against the way things are. If Gatsby's story is about America, so is Daisy's.

NOTES

Introduction

1. Terry Teachout, *The Skeptic* (New York: HarperCollins, 2002), 190–91.

2. Fitzgerald annotated and divided *The Outline of History* into forty sections, giving Sheilah Graham a novel or play to read corresponding to each period. See Sheilah Graham, *College of One: The Story of How F. Scott Fitzgerald Educated the Woman He Loved* (New York: Melville House, 2013), 89–90, 229.

3. Bronislaw Malinowski, *Argonauts of the Western Pacific* (Oxford: Benediction Classics, 2010), xv. Anthropology was important aside from its Faustian claims. T. S. Eliot took courses at Harvard during 1909–10 that connected "literary works through anthropology to supposedly primitive rituals." In 1919 Eliot wrote in *The Athenaeum*: "within the time of a brief generation it has become evident that some smattering of anthropology is as essential to culture as Rollin's Universal History." Robert Crawford, *Young Eliot: From St. Louis to "The Waste Land"* (New York: Farrar, Straus and Giroux, 2015), 117–18, 338.

4. Ludwig Wittgenstein, *Tractatus Logico-Philosophicus* (Mineola, NY: Dover Publications, 1999), 107.

5. Cited by Robert Beuka in *American Icon: Fitzgerald's "The Great Gatsby" in Critical and Cultural Context* (Rochester, NY: Camden House, 2011), 16–17.

6. Sarah E. Igo, "From Main Street to Mainstream: Middletown, Muncie, and 'Typical America.'" *Indiana Magazine of History* 101, no. 3 (2005): 239.

7. Lewis M. Dabney, *Edmund Wilson: A Life in Literature* (New York: Farrar, Straus and Giroux, 2005), 33.

8. "I had often urged writers to acquaint themselves with 'the realities of our contemporary life,' to apply themselves to 'the study of contemporary reality,' etc." Edmund Wilson, "The Literary Consequences of the Crash," in *Edmund Wilson:*

Literary Essays and Reviews of the 1920s and 30s, ed. Lewis M. Dabney (New York: Library of America, 2007), 403.

9. John Maynard Keynes, *The Economic Consequences of the Peace* (Seattle: Loki Publishing, n.d.), 10–14. Originally published in 1919; first American edition 1920.

10. F. Scott Fitzgerald, "Wait Till You Have Children of Your Own," in *F. Scott Fitzgerald: A Short Autobiography*, ed. James L. W. West III (New York: Scribner, 2011), 82.

11. Ibid., 80–81.

12. F. Scott Fitzgerald, "The Diamond as Big as the Ritz," in *The Short Stories of F. Scott Fitzgerald*, ed. Matthew J. Bruccoli (New York: Charles Scribner's Sons, 1989), 184.

13. H. W. Brands, *T. R.: The Last Romantic* (New York: Basic Books, 1997), 438–39, 457.

14. Josiah Royce, *The Philosophy of Josiah Royce*, ed. John K. Roth (Indianapolis: Hackett Publishing, 1982), 273.

15. Thomas Piketty, *Capital in the Twenty-First Century* (Cambridge, MA: Belknap Press of Harvard University Press, 2014), 272–73. See John Mullan, "How Much Money Is Enough," in *What Matters in Jane Austen* (New York: Bloomsbury Press, 2012), 196–210, for extensive discussion of affluence and its social effects in the novel.

16. F. Scott Fitzgerald, "Forging Ahead," in *The Basil, Josephine, and Gwen Stories*, ed. James L. W. West III (Cambridge: Cambridge University Press, 2009), 146.

17. Jürgen Osterhammel, *The Transformation of the World* (Princeton, NJ: Princeton University Press, 2014), 767, 777.

18. Crawford, *Young Eliot*, 182.

19. F. Scott Fitzgerald, "A Snobbish Story," in *The Basil, Josephine, and Gwen Stories*, 252.

20. Dwight Macdonald, *Masscult and Midcult* (New York: Partisan Review, 1961), 29.

21. Fitzgerald, "A Snobbish Story," 247, 251.

22. Ibid., 254.

23. Ibid., 191. Malcolm Cowley cites Sartre in *A Second Flowering: Works and Days of the Lost Generation* (New York: Viking, 1973), 83. Edward Mendelson cites Trilling in *Moral Agents: Eight Twentieth-Century American Writers* (New York: New York Review Books, 2015), 18.

24. America Past and Present Online—Report of the Vice Commission, Louisville, Kentucky. http://wps.ablongman.com/wps/media/objects/30/31419/primary sources6_22_1.html, accessed November 2014.

25. Crawford, *Young Eliot*, 199. The reference is to the love affair of T. S. Eliot and Emily Hale in 1914.

26. Walter Lippmann, "Upton Sinclair," in *Public Persons*, ed. Gilbert A. Harrison (New York: Liveright, 1976), 34.

27. F. Scott Fitzgerald, *The Great Gatsby*, ed. Matthew J. Bruccoli (Cambridge: Cambridge University Press, 1991), 19.

28. Annie Fellows Johnston, *The Little Colonel's Knight Comes Riding* (Boston: L. C. Page, 1907), 58–59.

29. Sigmund Freud, "Family Romances," in *The Freud Reader*, ed. Peter Gay (New York: W. W. Norton, 1989), 299.

Chapter 1

1. F. Scott Fitzgerald, *The Basil and Josephine Stories*, ed. Jackson R. Bryer and John Kuehl (New York: Collier Books, 1973), xxv.

2. Edith Wharton, "A Backward Glance," in *Edith Wharton: Novellas and Other Writings*, ed. Cynthia Griffin Wolff (New York: Library of America, 1990), 780. See the discussion of Wharton's reading of Darwin, Spencer, and others in Carol J. Singley, *A Historical Guide to Edith Wharton* (New York: Oxford University Press, 2003), 89–91. See also "Possible European Influences on American Theory," in Roscoe C. Hinkle, *Developments in American Sociological Theory, 1915–1950* (Albany: State University of New York Press, 1994), 273–300.

3. Walter Lippmann, *Public Opinion* (New York: Free Press, 1997), 14.

4. Ibid., 119.

5. Frances Kroll Ring, *Against the Current: As I Remember F. Scott Fitzgerald* (Berkeley, CA: Creative Arts Book Company, 1987), 65.

6. See Ronald Berman, *Fitzgerald's Mentors: Edmund Wilson, H. L. Mencken, and Gerald Murphy* (Tuscaloosa: University of Alabama Press, 2012), 1–10, 29–46.

7. Edmund Wilson, *Letters on Literature and Politics, 1912–1972*, ed. Elena Wilson (New York: Farrar, Straus and Giroux, 1977), 149–51.

8. Ibid., 44.

9. F. Scott Fitzgerald, *A Life in Letters*, ed. Matthew J. Bruccoli (New York: Simon and Schuster, 1994), 45.

10. B. F. Wilson, "F. Scott Fitzgerald Says: 'All Women over Thirty-Five Should Be Murdered,'" in *Conversations with F. Scott Fitzgerald*, ed. Matthew J. Bruccoli and Judith S. Baughman (Jackson: University Press of Mississippi, 2004), 57.

11. Fitzgerald, *A Life in Letters*, 436.

12. F. Scott Fitzgerald, *Tender Is the Night* (New York: Scribner, 2003) 57, 75.

13. Cited by Robert Beuka, *American Icon: Fitzgerald's "The Great Gatsby" in Critical and Cultural Context* (Rochester, NY: Camden House, 2011), 8.

14. Edmund Wilson, "F. Scott Fitzgerald," in *Edmund Wilson: Literary Essays and Reviews of the 1920s and 30s*, ed. Lewis M. Dabney (New York: Library of America, 2007), 32.

15. Wilson, "The Critic Who Does Not Exist," in *Edmund Wilson: Literary Essays and Reviews of the 1920s and 30s*, 305.

16. Wilson, "Dahlberg, Dos Passos and Wilder," in *Edmund Wilson: Literary Essays and Reviews of the 1920s and 30s*, 366. Wilson wrote the following in a letter to Walter Lippmann in early 1928: "Dos Passos . . . was saying to me the other day

that he thought the indifference to politics on the point of the literary and artistic people in New York was extremely sinister, because it was mere[ly] the first step in a process which subsequently involved the discarding of almost every other sort of interest, too." In *Letters on Literature and Politics, 1912–1972*, ed. Elena Wilson (New York: Farrar, Straus and Giroux, 1977), 145. See Lewis M. Dabney, "From Whitehead and Proust to Marx: *I Thought of Daisy* and *Axel's Castle*," in *Edmund Wilson: A Life in Literature* (New York: Farrar, Straus, and Giroux, 2005), 149–60.

17. "Citizen of the Union," in Wilson, *Literary Essays and Reviews of the 1920s and 1930s*, 343–44; "Dos Passos and the Social Revolution," in ibid., 354.

18. See Berman, *Fitzgerald's Mentors: Edmund Wilson, H. L. Mencken, and Gerald Murphy*, 2. There is an excellent account of Fitzgerald's ambivalent politics in Ring, *Against the Current*, 66: "Politically, Scott thought of himself as a liberal. He had voted for Roosevelt twice, but he was a passive, theoretical liberal, not an active one. I have a clear picture in mind of him lounging on the bed remarking that he would like to see a workers' revolution happen here, but he didn't want to be part of it."

19. Wilson, *Literary Essays and Reviews of the 1920s and 1930s*, 449, 468. See Wilson's "The Literary Class War," 438: "There is no question that the Gold-Wilder case marks definitely the eruption of the Marxist issues out of the literary circles of the radicals into the field of general criticism. It has now become plain that the economic crisis is to be accompanied by a literary one."

20. F. Scott Fitzgerald, *The Short Stories of F. Scott Fitzgerald*, ed. Matthew J. Bruccoli (New York: Simon and Schuster, 1989), 182.

21. Berman, *Fitzgerald's Mentors*, 11–19, 47–68.

22. Terry Teachout, *The Skeptic* (New York: HarperCollins, 2002), 238. Fitzgerald published in the *American Mercury*, and his letters indicate familiarity with its literary coverage. See Fitzgerald, *A Life in Letters*, 161, 170.

23. H. L. Mencken, *My Life as Author and Editor* (New York: Vintage Books, 1992), 239–40.

24. H. L. Mencken, "Psychologists in a Fog," in *A Mencken Chrestomathy* (New York: Alfred A. Knopf, 1967), 317–18.

25. H. L. Mencken, "How People Live," *American Mercury*, August 1933, 506–7.

26. Robert S. Lynd and Helen Merrell Lynd, *Middletown: A Study in Modern American Culture* (San Diego: Harcourt Brace, 1957), vi.

27. Ibid., 5–6.

28. Ibid., 199–200.

29. F. Scott Fitzgerald, *The Short Stories of F. Scott Fitzgerald*, ed. Matthew J. Bruccoli (New York: Charles Scribner's Sons, 1989), 54, 237, 619.

30. Correspondence of Edouard Jozan cited by Nancy Milford in *Zelda: A Biography* (New York: Harper and Row, 1970), 108–9.

31. F. Scott Fitzgerald, *The Basil, Josephine, and Gwen Stories*, ed. James L. W. West III (Cambridge: Cambridge University Press, 2009), 157.

32. Fitzgerald, *A Life in Letters*, 129–30.

33. F. Scott Fitzgerald, *F. Scott Fitzgerald on Authorship*, ed. Matthew J. Bruccoli with Judith S. Baughman (Columbia: University of South Carolina Press, 1996), 105–6.

34. Fitzgerald, *The Basil, Josephine, and Gwen Stories*, 163.

35. Hinkle, *Developments*, 173–74.

36. Ibid., 151–52.

37. F. Scott Fitzgerald, *Correspondence of F. Scott Fitzgerald*, ed. Matthew J. Bruccoli and Margaret M. Duggan (New York: Random House, 1980), 224–25.

38. Fitzgerald, *F. Scott Fitzgerald on Authorship*, 106.

39. Cited in Forrest G. Robinson, *Love's Story Told: A Life of Henry A. Murray* (Cambridge, MA: Harvard University Press, 1992), 140–43.

40. Ibid., 375.

41. Fitzgerald, *The Basil, Josephine, and Gwen Stories*, 60.

42. Robinson, *Love's Story Told*, 149.

43. Alfred North Whitehead, "The Romantic Reaction," in *Science and the Modern World* (New York: Macmillan, 1967), 92.

Chapter 2

1. F. Scott Fitzgerald, *The Beautiful and Damned*, ed. Alan Margolies (Oxford: Oxford University Press, 1998), 18.

2. F. Scott Fitzgerald, *Correspondence of F. Scott Fitzgerald*, ed. Matthew J. Bruccoli and Margaret M. Duggan (New York: Random House, 1980), 79.

3. Fitzgerald, *The Beautiful and Damned*, 328.

4. John Kuehl and Jackson R. Bryer, eds., *Dear Scott/Dear Max: The Fitzgerald-Perkins Correspondence* (New York: Charles Scribner's Sons, 1971), 111.

5. From the dust jacket of the 1922 edition of *The Beautiful and Damned*, in *The Romantic Egoists*, ed. Mathew J. Bruccoli, Scottie Fitzgerald Smith, and Jean P. Kerr (New York: Charles Scribner's Sons, 1974), 93. Max Perkins wrote to Fitzgerald before publication stating that he would follow his marketing suggestions; Fitzgerald responded that the passage would save the book "if anything can." In Kuehl and Bryer, *Dear Scott/Dear Max: The Fitzgerald-Perkins Correspondence*, 40, 57, 271. Louise Maunsell Field's review in the *New York Times* (March 5, 1922) found the novel's psychology "not particularly profound." That mattered less in her review than Fitzgerald's concentration on immorality.

6. F. Scott Fitzgerald, foreword to *The Short Stories of F. Scott Fitzgerald*, ed. Matthew J. Bruccoli (New York: Simon and Schuster, 1989), xi.

7. Cited by Matthew J. Bruccoli in *Scottie Fitzgerald: The Stewardship of Literary Memory* (Columbia: Thomas Cooper Library, University of South Carolina, 2007), 8, 9.

8. Sheilah Graham, *College of One* (New York: Melville House, 2013), 82, 134. See Christopher Hill on J. M. Morton as a Marxist historian whose work is best suited for those who have been badly taught and are new to the subject of working-class life:

"English History," *Labour Monthly* 20, no. 7 (1938): 449–52. He singles out the chapter in Morton described by Graham. Leslie Fiedler praised Fitzgerald's knowledge of "millionaires," "bourgeois," and "the lower middle class" in "Some Notes on F. Scott Fitzgerald," in *F. Scott Fitzgerald: A Collection of Critical Essays*, ed. Arthur Mizener (Englewood Cliffs, NJ: Prentice-Hall, 1963), 76.

9. Kuehl and Bryer, *Dear Scott/Dear Max: The Fitzgerald-Perkins Correspondence*, 84.

10. Edmund Wilson, "Prologue, 1952: Christian Gauss as a Teacher of Literature," in *Edmund Wilson: Literary Essays and Reviews of the 1920s and 30s*, ed. Lewis M. Dabney (New York: Library of America, 2007), 14, 20.

11. Fitzgerald, *Correspondence of F. Scott Fitzgerald*, 424.

12. "Fitzgerald and the Slick-Magazine Short Story: Testing Material for *Tender Is the Night*," in *F. Scott Fitzgerald's "Tender Is the Night": A Documentary Volume*, ed. Matthew J. Bruccoli and George Parker Anderson (Detroit: Gale, 2003), 96. Bruccoli added that Fitzgerald was uninterested in methodology: *Some Sort of Epic Grandeur: The Life of F. Scott Fitzgerald* (Columbia: University of South Carolina Press, 2002), 119.

13. Roscoe C. Hinkle, *Developments in American Sociological Theory, 1915–1950* (Albany: State University of New York Press, 1994), 19.

14. William James, *The Writings of William James*, ed. John J. McDermott (Chicago: University of Chicago Press, 1977), 473.

15. George Santayana, "William James," in *The Essential Santayana*, ed. Martin A. Coleman (Bloomington: Indiana University Press, 2009), 587.

16. Isaiah Berlin, *The Sense of Reality* (New York: Farrar, Straus and Giroux, 1996), 42–43.

17. Richard Overy, *The Morbid Age: Britain between the Wars* (London: Penguin Books, 2009), 107–8.

18. Ernest Hemingway, "Banal Story," in *The Short Stories* (New York: Scribner, 1995), 360–61.

19. Walter Lippmann, *Public Opinion* (New York: Free Press, 1997), 16–17. See H. L. Mencken on Upton Sinclair, who embraced chiropractic, deep breathing, crystal gazing, osteopathy, mental mastery, and the twilight sleep: *Prejudices: First, Second, and Third Series*, ed. Marion Elizabeth Rodgers (New York: Library of America, 2010), 424–25. Sinclair was also interested in many public issues like taxation and insurance and wrote credibly about them.

20. F. Scott Fitzgerald, "The Ice Palace," *Short Stories of F. Scott Fitzgerald*, 62.

21. Suzanne del Gizzo, "Ethnic Stereotyping," in *F. Scott Fitzgerald in Context*, ed. Bryant Mangum (Cambridge: Cambridge University Press, 2013), 226–27.

22. Overy, *Morbid Age*, 107.

23. Lionel Trilling, "William Dean Howells and the Roots of Modern Taste," in *The Moral Obligation to Be Intelligent*, ed. Leon Wieseltier (New York: Farrar, Straus and Giroux, 2000), 213.

24. Wilson, "F. Scott Fitzgerald," in *Edmund Wilson: Literary Essays and Reviews*

of the 1920s and 30s, 36. For implications of invoking the recent past see John Milton Cooper Jr., *Pivotal Decades: The United States, 1900–1920* (New York: W. W. Norton, 190), 365–66.

25. H. L. Mencken, "American Culture," in *A Mencken Chrestomathy* (New York: Alfred A. Knopf, 1967), 178–79. See Fitzgerald's description of the Park Avenue aristocracy in a letter to his daughter, November 10, 1936: Fitzgerald, *Correspondence of F. Scott Fitzgerald*, 461. Mencken argues the virtues of inherited aristocracy; Fitzgerald warns against the imitation of aristocracy.

26. Walter Lippmann, "H. L. Mencken," in *Public Persons*, ed. Gilbert A. Harrison (New York: Liveright, 1976), 78–79.

27. See the discussion of Prohibition and nativism in Michael A. Lerner, *Dry Manhattan* (Cambridge, MA: Harvard University Press, 2007), 96–101.

28. Fitzgerald, *The Beautiful and Damned*, 17.

29. F. Scott Fitzgerald, "The Scandal Detectives," in *The Basil, Josephine, and Gwen Stories*, 16.

30. F. Scott Fitzgerald, "My Generation," in *My Lost City: Personal Essays, 1920–1940*, ed. James L. W. West III (Cambridge: Cambridge University Press, 2005), 193.

31. F. Scott Fitzgerald, "The Diamond as Big as the Ritz," in *Short Stories of F. Scott Fitzgerald*, 201.

32. Fitzgerald, *Correspondence of F. Scott Fitzgerald*, 387,

33. Scott Donaldson, "Fitzgerald's Political Development," in *Fitzgerald and Hemingway* (New York: Columbia University Press 2009), 204–5.

34. See Matthew J. Bruccoli, *Some Sort of Epic Grandeur* (Columbia: University of South Carolina Press, 2002), 446–48, on Fitzgerald's specific understanding of Thomas Mann; and Donaldson, "Fitzgerald's Political Development," 204–5, for his general historical view of western Europe.

35. F. Scott Fitzgerald, "Dalyrimple Goes Wrong," in *Before Gatsby: The First Twenty-Six Stories*, ed. Matthew J. Bruccoli and Judith Baughman (Columbia: University of South Carolina Press, 2001), 62.

36. Fitzgerald, *The Beautiful and Damned*, 256.

37. See Bonnie Shannon McMullen, "'Can't We Put It in Writing?': Some Short Precursors to *Tender Is the Night*," in *Twenty-First-Century Readings of "Tender Is the Night*," ed. William Blazek and Laura Rattray (Liverpool: Liverpool University Press, 2007), 27.

38. Fitzgerald, *Correspondence of F. Scott Fitzgerald*, 79.

39. F. Scott Fitzgerald, "The Rich Boy," in *Short Stories of F. Scott Fitzgerald*, 336.

40. George Santayana, "The Birth of Reason," in *Essential Santayana*, 299.

41. Thomas Piketty, *Capital in the Twenty-First Century* (Cambridge, MA: Harvard University Press, 2014), 368.

42. F. Scott Fitzgerald, *The Great Gatsby*, ed. Matthew J. Bruccoli (Cambridge: Cambridge University Press, 1991), 27, 29.

43. F. Scott Fitzgerald, "A Man in the Way," in *The Pat Hobby Stories* (New York: Collier Macmillan, 1970), 13.

44. Jürgen Osterhammel, *The Transformation of the World: A Global History of the Nineteenth Century* (Princeton, NJ: Princeton University Press, 2014), 918.

45. Fitzgerald, "My Generation," 192–93. Fitzgerald states that he got the idea from Edmund Wilson.

46. Bruccoli, *Scottie Fitzgerald: The Stewardship of Literary Memory*, 9.

47. Robert S. Lynd, with the assistance of Alice C. Hanson, "The People as Consumers," in *Recent Social Trends in the United States, Report of the President's Research Committee on Social Trends*, 2 vols. (Westport, CT: Greenwood Press, 1970), 2: 866–67.

48. John Maynard Keynes, *The Economic Consequences of the Peace* (Seattle: Loki's Publishing, n.d.), 15.

49. See Richard Davenport-Hines, *Universal Man* (New York: Basic Books, 2015), 130–31. See also Robert Heilbroner, "The Man Who Made Us All Keynesians," *New York Times*, May 11, 1986, Book section, 1.

50. Berlin, *Sense of Reality*, 6.

51. Fitzgerald, *Correspondence of F. Scott Fitzgerald*, 25.

Chapter 3

1. Matthew J. Bruccoli and Judith S. Baughman, eds., *F. Scott Fitzgerald: A Life in Letters* (New York, Simon and Schuster, 1994), 402.

2. Ibid., 360.

3. F. Scott Fitzgerald, "My Generation," in *My Lost City: Personal Essays, 1920–1940*, ed. James L. W. West III (Cambridge: Cambridge University Press, 2005), 194.

4. Lloyd C. Hackl, *"Still Home to Me": F. Scott Fitzgerald and St. Paul, Minnesota* (Cambridge, MN: Adventure Publications, 1996), 29–30.

5. Fitzgerald, "My Generation," 194.

6. Edmund Wilson, "Mr. Rolfe," in *Edmund Wilson: Literary Essays and Reviews of the 1930s and 1940s*, ed. Lewis M. Dabney (New York: Library of America, 2007), 255.

7. George Orwell, "Such, Such Were the Joys," in *The Collected Essays, Journalism, and Letters of George Orwell*, vol. 4, *In Front of Your Nose: 1945–1950*, ed. Sonia Orwell and Ian Angus (New York: Harcourt, Brace and World, 1968), 360.

8. Lionel Trilling, "George Orwell and the Politics of Truth," in *The Moral Obligation to Be Intelligent*, ed. Leon Wieseltier (New York: Farrar, Straus, Giroux, 200), 283–87.

9. Jürgen Osterhammel, *The Transformation of the World* (Princeton, NJ: Princeton University Press, 2014), 767, 777. Literary history identifies modernity with books by Conrad, Shaw, Wells, and their contemporaries at the turn of century. H. L. Mencken explained the circulation of ideas at a different level: "and very much, indeed, has gone on since 1900. For one thing, the *Saturday Evening Post* has made

its unparalleled success, created its new type of American literature. . . . For another thing, the *Ladies' Home Journal*, once supreme in its field, has seen the rise of a swarm of imitators. . . . For a third thing, the all-fiction magazine of Munsey, Robert Bonner and Street & Smith has degenerated into so dubious a hussy that Munsey, a very moral man, must blush every time he thinks of it. For a fourth thing, the moving-picture craze has created an entirely new type of magazine, and it has elbowed many other types from the stands." Mencken emphasizes that social change was no longer the intellectual property of the "muck-raking magazine" but of entertainment. "The American Magazine," *Prejudices: First Series*, in *H. L. Mencken: Prejudices: First, Second, and Third Series*, ed. Marion Elizabeth Rodgers (New York: Library of America, 2010), 104. Published 1919.

10. F. Scott Fitzgerald, "The Captured Shadow," in *The Basil, Josephine, and Gwen Stories*, ed. James. L. W. West III (Cambridge: Cambridge University Press, 2009), 103.

11. Sheilah Graham and Gerold Frank, *Beloved Infidel: The Education of a Woman* (New York: Henry Holt, 1958), 261.

12. William Troy, "Scott Fitzgerald—the Authority of Failure," in *Fitzgerald: The Man and His Work*, ed. Alfred Kazin (New York: Collier, 1951), 189.

13. Ibid., 194.

14. Sigmund Freud, *Civilization and Its Discontents*, ed. James Strachey (New York: W. W. Norton, 1961), 97–98.

15. F. Scott Fitzgerald, *This Side of Paradise*, ed. James L. W. West III (Cambridge: Cambridge University Press, 1995), 220. According to Peter Gay, ed., *The Freud Reader* (New York: W. W. Norton, 1989), 722, *Civilization and Its Discontents* summarizes Freud's "long-held theories of culture."

16. Fitzgerald, *A Life in Letters*, 460.

17. Fitzgerald, *This Side of Paradise*, 142–43.

18. H. L. Mencken, *The American Language* (New York: Alfred A. Knopf, 2000), 300–311).

19. Fitzgerald, *This Side of Paradise*, 65.

20. George Herbert Mead, "The Social Foundations and Functions of Thought and Communication," in *Classical American Philosophy*, ed. John J. Stuhr (New York: Oxford University Press, 1987), 452–54.

21. John Dewey, "The School and Social Progress," in *The Philosophy of John Dewey*, ed. John J. McDermott (Chicago: University of Chicago Press, 1984), 458.

22. George Santayana, *The Genteel Tradition*, ed. Douglas L. Wilson (Lincoln: University of Nebraska Press, 1998), 38–40.

23. Ibid., 163–64.

24. Ibid., 193.

25. Edmund Wilson, *I Thought of Daisy* (Baltimore: Penguin Books, 1963), 200.

26. Cited by Matthew J. Bruccoli in *Some Sort of Epic Grandeur: The Life of F. Scott Fitzgerald* (Columbia: University of South Carolina Press, 2002), 390.

27. F. Scott Fitzgerald, introduction to *The Basil, Josephine, and Gwen Stories*, xiii. See John T. Irwin, *F. Scott Fitzgerald's Fiction: "An Almost Theatrical Innocence"* (Baltimore: Johns Hopkins University Press, 2014), 103–9.

28. Bruccoli, *Some Sort of Epic Grandeur*, 264. See Nancy Milford, *Zelda: A Biography* (New York: Harper and Row, 1970), 149. "In the winter of 1928–1929 Zelda began writing the first in a series of short stories that dealt with the lives of six young women."

29. Milford, *Zelda*, 149.

30. Sigmund Freud, "The Ego and the Id," in *The Freud Reader*, ed. Peter Gay (New York: W. W. Norton, 1989), 643.

31. Fitzgerald, *The Basil, Josephine, and Gwen Stories*, 131.

32. See Frederick Lewis Allen, *Only Yesterday* (New York: Perennial Library, 2000), 78–79.

33. H. L. Mencken, "The Fruits of Comstockery," in *A Mencken Chrestomathy* (New York: Alfred A. Knopf, 1967), 352.

34. H. L. Mencken, "The Triumph of Idealism," in *Prejudices: Second Series* (London: Jonathan Cape, 1921), 226–27.

35. F. Scott Fitzgerald, *Correspondence of F. Scott Fitzgerald*, ed. Matthew J. Bruccoli and Margaret M. Duggan (New York: Random House, 1980), 54, 70.

36. Lisa McGirr, *The War on Alcohol* (New York: W. W. Norton, 2016), 118.

37. Michael A. Lerner, *Dry Manhattan* (Cambridge, MA: Harvard University Press, 2007), 173–76.

38. Alan Ryan, *John Dewey and the High Tide of American Liberalism* (New York: W. W. Norton, 1995), 318–19.

39. Lionel Trilling, "D. H. Lawrence: A Neglected Aspect," in *Speaking of Literature and Society* (New York: Harcourt Brace Jovanovich, 1980), 39.

40. F. Scott Fitzgerald, *Before Gatsby: The First Twenty-Six Stories* (Columbia: University of South Carolina Press, 2001), 295.

41. H. L. Mencken, *Notes on Democracy*, ed. Marion Elizabeth Rodgers (New York: Dissident Books, 2009), 63.

42. Fitzgerald, *The Basil, Josephine, and Gwen Stories*, 136.

43. Fitzgerald, *Before Gatsby*, 356.

44. Alexis de Tocqueville, *Democracy in America*, 2 vols., ed. Henry Reeve (New York: Alfred A. Knopf, 1945), 2: 55: "There is hardly a pioneer's hut that does not contain a few odd volumes of Shakespeare. I remember that I read the feudal drama of *Henry V* for the first time in a log cabin."

45. H. L. Mencken, "The Sahara of the Bozart," in *Prejudices: Second Series* (London: Jonathan Cape, 1921), 155. Earlier forms of this essay were published before Fitzgerald's story.

46. Ibid., 142–44. Mencken described what would become Fitzgerald's southern narrative: the escape from south to north and return.

47. Edmund Wilson, "Why Do People Read Detective Stories?" in *Literary Essays and Reviews of the 1930s and 40s*, 661.

48. George Orwell, "Raffles and Miss Blandish," in *The Collected Essays, Journalism, and Letters of George Orwell*, vol. 3, *As I Please: 1943–1945*, ed. Sonia Orwell and Ian Angus (New York: Harcourt, Brace and World, 1968), 212, 214. Movies about Raffles appeared in 1917, 1925, 1930, and 1940. Fitzgerald worked briefly on the script of the 1939 version starring David Niven. See Bruccoli, *Some Sort of Epic Grandeur*, 466.

49. Robert S. Lynd and Helen Merrell Lynd, *Middletown: A Study in American Culture* (San Diego: Harcourt Brace, 1957), 197–98.

50. Fitzgerald, *Before Gatsby*, 59, 62, 63, 65, 67.

51. Osterhammel, *Transformation of the World*, 762. Emphasis added.

Chapter 4

1. Richard D. Altick, The Presence of the Present: Topics of the Day in the Victorian Novel (Columbus: Ohio State University Press, 1991), 626.

2. Thomas Piketty, Capital in the Twenty-First Century (Cambridge, MA: Belknap Press of Harvard University Press, 2014), 293.

3. Ibid., 415.

4. Fitzgerald wrote to his daughter, Scottie, that "Park Avenue girls are hard, aren't they? My own taste ran to kinder people, but they are usually the daughters of 'up-and-coming' men and, in a way the inevitable offspring of the type. It is Yankee push to its last degree." F. Scott Fitzgerald, Correspondence of F. Scott Fitzgerald, ed. Matthew J. Bruccoli and Margaret M. Duggan (New York: Random House, 1980), 461.

5. Steve Fraser, The Age of Acquiescence (New York: Little, Brown, 2015), 170–72.

6. Horatio Alger, introduction to Ragged Dick and Struggling Upward, ed. Carl Bode (New York: Penguin, 1985), i.

7. George Santayana, Character and Opinion in the United States (Garden City, NY: Doubleday, 1956), 115.

8. John Maynard Keynes, The Economic Consequences of the Peace (Seattle: Loki's Publishing, n.d.) 114. The book was published in England in 1919 and in the United States in 1920.

9. See Lionel Trilling, "The Princess Casamassima," in The Moral Obligation to be Intelligent, ed. Leon Wieseltier (New York: Farrar, Straus, Giroux, 2000), 132–35. For the cost of middle-class commodities in Balzac see Ronald Berman, "Analogies and Realities in Père Goriot," Novel 3 (Fall 1969): 7–16.

10. Gary Falk, Louisville Remembered (Charleston, SC: History Press, 2009), 47.

11. Scott Donaldson, "Money and Marriage in Fitzgerald's Stories," in Fitzgerald and Hemingway: Works and Days (New York: Columbia University Press, 2009), 107–18.

12. Piketty, Capital in the Twenty-First Century, 272–73.

13. Michael McGerr, A Fierce Discontent: The Rise and Fall of the Progressive Movement in America, 1870–1920 (New York: Free Press, 2003), 13. See the informative passages on "Scott's social-consciousness pattern" in Sheilah Graham, College of One (New York: Melville House, 2013), 136–37. Fitzgerald admired Frank Norris, John Reed, and Upton Sinclair; he recommended economic studies of the Progressive Era including Bouck White's life of a robber baron, The Book of Daniel Drew (1910).

14. See Kirk Curnutt's discussion of consumption and style in The Cambridge Introduction to F. Scott Fitzgerald (Cambridge: Cambridge University Press, 2007), 34–38.

15. F. Scott Fitzgerald, The Great Gatsby, ed. Matthew J. Bruccoli (Cambridge: Cambridge University Press, 1991), 131.

16. F. Scott Fitzgerald, "The Diamond as Big as the Ritz," in The Short Stories of F. Scott Fitzgerald, ed. Matthew J. Bruccoli (New York: Simon and Schuster, 1989), 184.

17. H. L. Mencken, "To Him That Hath," in A Mencken Chrestomathy (New York: Alfred A. Knopf, 1967), 293. See also "The Anglo-Saxon," 169–77.

18. Cited by Richard Davenport-Hines, Universal Man: The Lives of John Maynard Keynes (New York: Basic Books, 2015), 10.

19. Piketty, Capital in the Twenty-First Century, 419.

20. H. L. Mencken, "The National Letters," in Prejudices: Second Series (London: Jonathan Cape, 1921), 67.

21. H. L. Mencken, Notes on Democracy, ed. Marion Elizabeth Rodgers (New York: Dissident Books, 2009), 52.

22. Walter Lippmann, Public Opinion (New York: Free Press, 1997), 72.

23. Philipp Blom, The Vertigo Years: Europe, 1900–1914 (New York: Basic Books, 2008), 285.

24. Martin Birnbaum, Catalogue of an Exhibition of Contemporary Graphic Art in Hungary, Bohemia, and Austria (Chicago: Art Institute of Chicago, 1914), 10, 11. Recent work on Cézanne emphasizes his traditionalism. See excerpts from his letters urging study of the past in Francoise Cachin, "A Century of Cézanne Criticism I: From 1865–1906," in Cézanne, ed. Francoise Cachin, Isabelle Cahn, Walter Feilchenfeldt, Henri Loyette, and Joseph J. Rishel (Philadelphia: Harry N. Abrams, 1996), 42. William Morris was evidently a target of convenience, chosen despite the evidence of his life and his art. He remains a presence, and there are enormous numbers of reproductions of his work currently sold by Amazon Books.

25. Fitzgerald, The Basil, Josephine, and Gwen Stories, 245. Further references to this story in parentheses are in my text.

26. For commodities in the Josephine stories see Mary McAleer Balkun, "One Cannot Both Spend and Have," in F. Scott Fitzgerald in the Twenty-First Century, ed. Jackson R. Bryer, Ruth Prigozy, and Milton R. Stern (Tuscaloosa: University of Alabama Press, 2003), 121–38.

27. Catalogue of an Exhibition of Modern Painting by Albert Bloch of Munich (Chicago: Art Institute of Chicago, 1915), 6.

28. George Santayana, "Public Opinion," in The Essential Santayana, ed. Martin A. Coleman (Bloomington: Indiana University Press, 2009), 462.

29. Ruth Prigozy, "Fitzgerald's Flappers and Flapper Films of the Jazz Age: Behind the Morality," in A Historical Guide to F. Scott Fitzgerald, ed. Kirk Curnutt (Oxford: Oxford University Press, 2004), 139.

30. Ivan Caryll, Chin-Chin: A Musical Fantasy in Three Acts (New York: Chappell, 1914), 17.

31. F. Scott Fitzgerald, "The Offshore Pirate," in The Short Stories of F. Scott Fitzgerald, ed. Matthew J. Bruccoli (New York: Scribner, 1989), 81.

32. Josiah Royce, The Philosophy of Josiah Royce, ed. John K. Roth (Indianapolis: Hackett Publishing, 1982), 273.

33. Ibid., 274.

34. Simmel published The Metropolis and Mental Life in 1903.

35. Charlene Haddock Seigfried, "James: Sympathetic Apprehension of the Point of View of the Other," in Classical American Pragmatism, ed. Sandra B. Rosenthal, Carl R. Hausman, and Douglas R. Anderson (Urbana: University of Illinois Press, 1999), 85.

36. Robert W. Snyder, The Voice of the City (Chicago: Ivan R. Dee, 1989), 110. Snyder cites Raymond Williams on characters who "simulate but not affirm human identity."

37. Edmund Wilson, Edmund Wilson: Literary Essays and Reviews of the 1920s and 1930s, ed. Lewis M. Dabney (New York: Library of America, 2007), 716.

38. Snyder, Voice of the City, 79.

39. Ibid., 54.

40. Ibid., 145. The Little Theatre movement was supported by donors in Chicago. Over the ten-year period named by Fitzgerald, its leading performers went to the Broadway stage, vaudeville, silent film, radio, and, eventually, the talkies. Vaudeville encompassed nearly all aspects of show business. For a firsthand account of the dispersion of talent from the provinces see George Burns, All My Best Friends (New York: G. P. Putnam's Sons, 1989), 40–64.

41. F. Scott Fitzgerald, "Echoes of the Jazz Age," in My Lost City, ed. James. L. W. West III (Cambridge: Cambridge University Press, 2005), 133–34.

42. Walter Lippmann, "Sinclair Lewis," in Public Persons, ed. Gilbert A. Harrison (New York: Liveright, 1976), 85, 86.

43. James L. W. West III, The Perfect Hour (New York: Random House, 2006), 126.

44. Fitzgerald, "Echoes of the Jazz Age," 131, 132.

Chapter 5

1. See Jonathan N. Barron, "Teaching Regionalism and Class in The Great Gatsby," in Approaches to Teaching Fitzgerald's "The Great Gatsby," ed. Jackson R. Bryer and

Nancy P. VanArsdale (New York: MLA, 2009), 65: "In Mississippi, my students often have a hard time imagining Louisville, so far to their north, as part of the South."

2. Lewis Dabney, *Edmund Wilson: A Life in Literature* (New York: Farrar, Straus and Giroux, 2005), 55, 67.

3. Edmund Wilson, *Letters on Literature and Politics, 1912–1972*, ed. Elena Wilson (New York: Farrar, Straus and Giroux, 1977), 29, 32.

4. Andrew Turnbull, *Scott Fitzgerald* (New York: Charles Scribner's Sons, 1962), 81, 83.

5. F. Scott Fitzgerald, *The Great Gatsby*, ed. Matthew J. Bruccoli (Cambridge: Cambridge University Press, 1991), 116. Future references in text.

6. Robert Beuka, *SuburbiaNation* (New York: Palgrave Macmillan, 2004), 30. See Fitzgerald's description of "Camp Hooker" in *The Beautiful and Damned*, ed. Alan Margolies (Oxford: Oxford University Press, 1998), 248–49.

7. Gary Falk, *Louisville Remembered* (Charleston, SC: History Press, 2009), 47–48, 112.

8. Ibid., 143.

9. Ibid., 132–33.

10. See Jürgen Osterhammel, *The Transformation of the World: A Global History of the Nineteenth Century* (Princeton, NJ: Princeton University Press, 2014), 777.

11. Local archives include the Conrad-Caldwell House Museum, the photo collection of the University of Louisville, and that of the Camp Zachary Taylor Historical Society. See Falk, *Louisville Remembered*; David Dominé and Ronald Lew Harris, *Old Louisville*, Images of America (Charleston, SC: Arcadia Publishing, 2010).

12. Dominé and Harris, *Old Louisville*, 40: "Built in 1885, the Fourth Avenue home of vinegar manufacturer Vernon Price sported a distinct facade covered in rough polychrome fieldstone with squared columns and carved capitals supporting the front porch. The attention to details carries over to the interior, where hand-carved fireplace mantels, elaborate millwork, and stained glass adorn the mansion's 18 rooms."

13. "Appreciating Edith Wharton's Other Career," *New York Times*, August 30, 2012, Home and Garden section.

14. Robert S. Lynd and Helen Merrell Lynd, *Middletown: A Study in Modern American Culture* (San Diego: Harcourt Brace, 1957), 52.

15. Joseph Ravaisou is cited by Alex Danchev, *Cézanne: A Life* (New York: Pantheon, 2012), 328–29.

16. Wilson, *Letters on Literature and Politics, 1912–1972*, 44. See the section on "nice" girls and the codes governing them in Frederick Lewis Allen, *Only Yesterday* (New York: HarperCollins Perennial, 2000), 76–81.

17. Wilson, *Letters on Literature and Politics*, 32. The letter mentions the family of David Hamilton of Grosse Pointe Farms but does not identify individuals. Wilson notes only that their social group is "exceptional in America."

18. F. Scott Fitzgerald, *The Short Stories of F. Scott Fitzgerald*, ed. Matthew J. Bruccoli (New York: Simon and Schuster, 1989), 51, 87.

19. Anatole France, *The Revolt of the Angels*, trans. Emilie Jackson (New York: Dodd, Mead, 1922), 9. According to Mencken, the novel was in itself a guide to modern times, praising "the heresies of Darwin, Huxley, Spencer, Weismann, Harnack, Strauss, Renan and the rest." *H. L. Mencken's Smart Set Criticism*, ed. William H. Nolte (Washington, DC: Gateway, 1987), 262. Becky Sharp tosses Johnson's dictionary out of a window; Ardita throws *The Revolt of the Angels* at her uncle.

20. H. L. Mencken, "The Feminine Mind," in *A Mencken Chrestomathy* (New York: Alfred A. Knopf, 1967), 27. Revised 1922.

21. Ibid., 26.

22. H. L. Mencken, "A Loss to Romance," in *A Mencken Chrestomathy*, 57.

23. In his letter of January 1918, Bishop discussed his own reading, his army experiences, and Fitzgerald's first novel, stating twice that sociology in the novel was a mistake. He thought that sensibility mattered "more than all the sociology in the world." In *Correspondence of F. Scott Fitzgerald*, ed. Matthew J. Bruccoli and Margaret M. Duggan (New York: Random House, 1980), 25.

24. F. Scott Fitzgerald, *The Beautiful and Damned*, ed. Alan Margolies (Oxford: Oxford University Press, 1998), 256. See the introduction, xvi–xvii, for "literary naturalism" in the novel.

25. Michael McGerr, *A Fierce Discontent: The Rise and Fall of the Progressive Movement in America, 1870–1920* (New York: Free Press, 2003), 13. In 1917, Edmund Wilson wrote of his wartime experiences that he felt pity but not empathy for "'the poor white trash' of the South." He wrote that he reserved his feelings for his own class (*Letters on Literature and Politics, 1912–1972*, 36). In 1926, Fitzgerald described women of his own class and below them: "Of a far better type are the working girls of the middle classes, the thousands of young women who are the power behind some stupid man in a thousand offices all over the United States . . . she is a far higher type of woman than our colleges or our country clubs produce" ("Wait Till You Have Children of Your Own!"), in *F. Scott Fitzgerald: A Short Autobiography*, ed. James L. W. West III (New York: Scribner, 2011), 82–83.

26. Annie Fellows Johnston, *The Little Colonel at Boarding-School* (Boston: L. C. Page, 1909), 15.

27. Sigmund Freud, *Civilization and Its Discontents*, ed. James Strachey (New York: W. W. Norton, 1989), 31.

28. See Dominé and Harris, *Old Louisville*, 52, for photographs and (limited) information on publication and translation of Johnston's *Little Colonel* and *Two Little Knights of Kentucky* series.

29. Jane Tompkins, *Sensational Designs: The Cultural Work of American Fiction, 1790–1860* (New York: Oxford University Press, 1985), 126–27. Cited by Thomas

Morgan in "Sentimentalizing Daisy for the Screen," *F. Scott Fitzgerald Review* 12 (2014): 15. Morgan's useful essay discusses additions to and evasions of Fitzgerald's text by Hollywood.

30. In a 1929 letter to Hamilton Basso, Wilson stated that Fitzgerald's "prose and dramatic sense" were better than his own. *Letters on Literature and Politics, 1912–1972*, 173. Lewis Dabney states in *Edmund Wilson: A Life in Literature* that it was almost impossible for Wilson to recognize that he "was a better writer about literary and historical figures than of fiction" (113).

31. Edmund Wilson, *The Higher Jazz*, ed. Neale Reinitz (Iowa City: University of Iowa Press, 1998), 149.

32. Dabney, *Edmund Wilson: A Life in Literature*, 148.

33. Edmund Wilson, *I Thought of Daisy* (Baltimore: Penguin Books, 1963), 59.

34. Ibid., 215.

35. See Matthew J. Bruccoli, *F. Scott Fitzgerald's "The Great Gatsby": A Documentary Volume*, Dictionary of Literary Biography 219 (Detroit: Gale, 2000), 198–203.

36. See Robert Beuka, *American Icon: Fitzgerald's "The Great Gatsby" in Critical and Cultural Context* (Rochester, NY: Camden House, 2011), 127.

37. John Dewey, "Search for the Great Community," in *The Philosophy of John Dewey*, ed. John J. McDermott (Chicago: University of Chicago Press, 1981), 624–25.

38. Bertrand Russell, *The Analysis of Mind* (London: Routledge, 2002) 132. See Niklas Salmose, "Reading Nostalgia: Textual Memory in *The Great Gatsby*," *F. Scott Fitzgerald Review* 12 (2014): 83–84, for an analysis of memory and modernism.

39. Fitzgerald, *The Great Gatsby*, 117.

40. Lionel Trilling, "The Morality of Inertia," in *The Moral Obligation to Be Intelligent*, ed. Leon Wieseltier (New York: Farrar, Straus and Giroux, 2000), 332, 334, 337.

41. Sigmund Freud, *The Freud Reader*, ed. Peter Gay (New York: W. W. Norton, 1989). Gay notes (297) that "Romances" in this essay of 1908 should be understood as "novels." The essay bears on *The Great Gatsby* since it is about "getting free from the parents of whom he now has a low opinion and of replacing them by others, who as a rule, are of higher social standing" (299).

42. Nancy J. Scott, *Georgia O'Keeffe* (London: Reaktion Books, 2015), 96. Cited from Georgia O'Keeffe statement in *Alfred Stieglitz Presents One Hundred Pictures*, exhibition of 1923.

43. Lionel Trilling thought it impossible to escape "from the growing power of culture to control us by seduction or coercion." There was, he said, no "possibility that a private conscience or individual will could resists its surrounding culture." Cited by Edward Mendelson, "Sages: Lionel Trilling," in *Moral Agents: Eight Twentieth-Century American Writers* (New York: New York Review Books, 2015), 18.

BIBLIOGRAPHY

Alger, Horatio. *Ragged Dick and Struggling Upward*. Edited by Carl Bode. New York: Penguin, 1985.

Allen, Frederick Lewis. *Only Yesterday*. New York: Perennial Library, 2000.

America Past and Present Online.

Balkun, Mary McAleer. "'One Cannot Both Spend and Have': The Economics of Gender in Fitzgerald's Josephine Stories." In *F. Scott Fitzgerald in the Twenty-First Century*, edited by Jackson Bryer, Ruth Prigozy, and Milton R. Stern, 121–38. Tuscaloosa: University of Alabama Press, 2003.

Barron, Jonathan N. "Teaching Regionalism and Class in *The Great Gatsby*." In *Approaches to Teaching Fitzgerald's "The Great Gatsby*,*"* edited by Jackson R. Bryer and Nancy P. VanArsdale. New York: MLA, 2009.

Berlin, Isaiah. *The Sense of Reality*. New York: Farrar, Straus and Giroux, 1996.

Berman, Ronald. "Analogies and Realities in *Père Goriot*." *Novel* 3 (Fall 1969).

———. *Fitzgerald's Mentors: Edmund Wilson, H. L. Mencken, and Gerald Murphy*. Tuscaloosa: University of Alabama Press, 2012.

Beuka, Robert. *American Icon: Fitzgerald's "The Great Gatsby" in Critical and Cultural Context*. Rochester, NY: Camden House, 2011.

———. "Magazines." In *F. Scott Fitzgerald in Context*, edited by Bryant Mangum, 283–92. Cambridge: Cambridge University Press, 2013.

———. *SuburbiaNation*. New York: Palgrave Macmillan, 2004.

Birnbaum, Martin. *Catalogue of an Exhibition of Contemporary Graphic Art in Hungary, Bohemia, and Austria*. Chicago: Art Institute of Chicago, 1914.

Blom, Philipp. *The Vertigo Years: Europe, 1900–1914*. New York: Basic Books, 2008.

Brands, H. W. *T. R.: The Last Romantic*. New York: Basic Books, 1997.

Bruccoli, Matthew J. *Scottie Fitzgerald: The Stewardship of Literary Memory*. Columbia: Thomas Cooper Library, University of South Carolina, 2007.

———. *Some Sort of Epic Grandeur: The Life of F. Scott Fitzgerald*. Columbia: University of South Carolina Press, 2002.

Bruccoli, Matthew J., ed. *F. Scott Fitzgerald's* The Great Gatsby: *A Documentary Volume*. Dictionary of Literary Biography 219. Detroit: Gale, 2000.

Bruccoli, Matthew J., and George Parker Anderson, eds. *F. Scott Fitzgerald's "Tender Is the Night": A Documentary Volume*. Detroit: Gale, 2003.

Bruccoli, Matthew J., and Judith S. Baughman, eds. *Conversations with F. Scott Fitzgerald*. Jackson: University Press of Mississippi, 2004.

Cachin, Francoise, Isabelle Cahn, Walter Fielchenfeldt, Henri Loyette, and Joseph J. Rishel, eds. *Cézanne*. Philadelphia: Harry N. Abrams, 1996.

Caryll, Ivan. *Chin-Chin: A Musical Fantasy in Three Acts*. New York: Chappell, 1914.

Catalogue of an Exhibition of Modern Painting by Albert Bloch of Munich. Chicago: Art Institute of Chicago, 1915.

Cooper, John Milton. *Pivotal Decades: The United States, 1900–1920*. New York: W. W. Norton, 1990.

Cowley, Malcolm. *A Second Flowering: Works and Days of the Lost Generation*. New York: Viking, 1973.

Crawford, Robert. *Young Eliot: From St. Louis to "The Waste Land."* New York: Farrar, Straus and Giroux, 2015.

Curnutt, Kirk. *The Cambridge Introduction to F. Scott Fitzgerald*. Cambridge: Cambridge University Press, 2007.

Dabney, Lewis M. *Edmund Wilson: A Life in Literature*. New York: Farrar, Straus and Giroux, 2005.

Danchev, Alex. *Cézanne: A Life*. New York: Pantheon, 2012.

Davenport-Hines, Richard. *Universal Man: The Lives of John Maynard Keynes*. New York: Basic Books, 2015.

Del Gizzo, Suzanne. "Ethnic Stereotyping." In *F. Scott Fitzgerald in Context*, edited by Bryant Mangum, 224–33. Cambridge: Cambridge University Press, 2013.

Dewey, John. *The Philosophy of John Dewey*. Edited by John J. McDermott. Chicago: University of Chicago Press, 1984.

Dominé, David, and Ronald Lew Harris. *Old Louisville*. Images of America. Charleston, SC: Arcadia Publishing, 2010.

Donaldson, Scott. *Fitzgerald and Hemingway: Works and Days*. New York: Columbia University Press, 2009.

Falk, Gary. *Louisville Remembered*. Charleston, SC: History Press, 2009.

Fitzgerald, F. Scott. *The Basil and Josephine Stories*. Edited by Jackson R. Bryer and John Kuehl. New York: Collier Macmillan, 1973.

———. *The Basil, Josephine, and Gwen Stories*. Edited by James L. W. West III. Cambridge: Cambridge University Press, 2009.

———. *The Beautiful and Damned*. Edited by Alan Margolies. Oxford: Oxford University Press, 1998.

———. *Before Gatsby: The First Twenty-Six Stories*. Edited by Matthew J. Bruccoli. Columbia: University of South Carolina Press, 2001.

———. *Correspondence of F. Scott Fitzgerald*. Edited by Matthew J. Bruccoli and Margaret M. Duggan. New York: Random House, 1980.

———. *F. Scott Fitzgerald: A Short Autobiography*. Edited by James L. W. West III. New York: Scribner, 2011.

———. *F. Scott Fitzgerald on Authorship*. Edited by Mathew J. Bruccoli and Judith S. Baughman. Columbia: University of South Carolina Press, 1996.

———. *The Great Gatsby*. Edited by Matthew J. Bruccoli. Cambridge: Cambridge University Press, 1991.

———. *A Life in Letters*. Edited by Matthew J. Bruccoli. New York: Simon and Schuster, 1994.

———. *My Lost City: Personal Essays, 1920–1940*. Edited by James L. W. West III. Cambridge: Cambridge University Press, 2005.

———. *The Pat Hobby Stories*. New York: Collier Macmillan, 1970.

———. *The Short Stories of F. Scott Fitzgerald*. Edited by Matthew J Bruccoli. New York: Simon and Schuster, 1989.

———. *Tender Is the Night*. New York: Scribner, 2003.

———. *This Side of Paradise*. Edited by James. L. G. West III. Cambridge: Cambridge University Press, 1995.

France, Anatole. *The Revolt of the Angels*. Translated by Emilie Jackson. New York: Dodd, Mead, 1922.

Fraser, Steve. *The Age of Acquiescence*. New York: Little, Brown, 2015.

Freud, Sigmund. *Civilization and Its Discontents*. Edited by James Strachey. New York: W. W. Norton, 1989.

———. *The Freud Reader*. Edited by Peter Gay. New York: W. W. Norton, 1989.

Graham, Sheilah. *College of One*. New York: Melville House, 2013.

Graham, Sheilah, and Gerold Frank. *Beloved Infidel: The Education of a Woman*. New York: Henry Holt, 1958.

Hackl, Lloyd C. *"Still Home to Me": F. Scott Fitzgerald and St. Paul, Minnesota*. Cambridge, MN: Adventure Publications, 1996.

Hemingway, Ernest. *The Short Stories*. New York: Scribner, 1995.

Hinkle, Roscoe C. *Developments in American Sociological Theory, 1915–1950*. Albany: State University of New York Press, 1994.

Igo, Sarah E. "From Main Street to Mainstream: Middletown, Muncie, and 'Typical America.'" *Indiana Magazine of History* 101, no. 3 (2005): 239–66.

Irwin, John T. *F. Scott Fitzgerald's Fiction: "An Almost Theatrical Innocence."* Baltimore: Johns Hopkins University Press, 2014.

James, William. *The Writings of William James*. Edited by John J. McDermott. Chicago: University of Chicago Press, 1977.

Johnston, Annie Fellows. *The Little Colonel at Boarding-School*. Boston: L. C. Page, 1909.

——. *The Little Colonel's Knight Comes Riding.* Boston: L. C. Page, 1907.

Keynes, John Maynard. *The Economic Consequences of the Peace.* Seattle: Loki's Publications, n.d. Originally published 1919.

Kuehl, John, and Jackson Bryer, eds. *Dear Scott/Dear Max: The Fitzgerald-Perkins Correspondence.* New York: Charles Scribner's Sons, 1971.

Lerner, Michael A. *Dry Manhattan.* Cambridge, MA: Harvard University Press, 2007.

Le Vot, André. *F. Scott Fitzgerald: A Biography.* Translated by William Byron. Garden City, NY: Doubleday, 1983.

Lippmann, Walter. *Public Opinion.* New York: Free Press, 1997.

——. *Public Persons.* Edited by Gilbert A. Harrison. New York: Liveright, 1976.

Lynd, Robert S., and Alice G. Hanson, "The People as Consumers." In *Recent Social Trends in the United States: Report of the President's Committee on Social Trends.* 2 vols. Westport, CT: Greenwood Press, 1970.

Lynd, Robert S., and Helen Merrell Lynd. *Middletown: A Study in Modern American Culture.* San Diego: Harcourt Brace, 1957.

Macdonald, Dwight. *Masscult and Midcult.* New York: Partisan Review, 1961.

Malinowski, Bronislaw. *Argonauts of the Western Pacific.* Oxford: Benediction Classics, 2010.

Marchand, Roland. *Advertising the American Dream.* Berkeley: University of California Press, 1986.

McGerr, Michael. *A Fierce Discontent: The Rise and Fall of the Progressive Movement in America, 1870–1920.* New York: Free Press, 2003.

McGirr, Lisa. *The War on Alcohol.* New York: W. W. Norton, 2016.

Mead, George Herbert. "The Social Foundations and Functions of Thought and Communication." In *Classical American Philosophy*, edited by John. J. Stuhr. New York: Oxford University Press, 1987.

Mencken, H. L. *The American Language.* New York: Alfred A. Knopf, 2000.

——. "How People Live." *American Mercury*, August 1933.

——. *A Mencken Chrestomathy.* New York: Alfred A. Knopf, 1967.

——. *My Life as Author and Editor.* New York: Vintage, 1992.

——. *Notes on Democracy.* Edited by Marion Elizabeth Rodgers. New York: Dissident Books, 2009.

——. *Prejudices: First, Second, and Third Series.* Edited by Marion Elizabeth Rodgers. New York: Library of America, 2010.

——. *Prejudices: Second Series.* London: Jonathan Cape, 1921.

Mendelson, Edward. *Moral Agents: Eight Twentieth-Century Writers.* New York: New York Review Books, 2015.

Milford, Nancy. *Zelda: A Biography.* New York: Harper and Row, 1970.

Morgan, Thomas, "Sentimentalizing Daisy for the Screen." *F. Scott Fitzgerald Review* 12 (2014): 13–31.

Orwell, George. *The Collected Essays, Journalism, and Letters of George Orwell.* Vols.

3 and 4. Edited by Sonia Orwell and Ian Angus. New York: Harcourt, Brace and World, 1968.

Osterhammel, Jürgen. *The Transformation of the World: A Global History of the Nineteenth Century.* Princeton, NJ: Princeton University Press, 2014.

Overy, Richard. *The Morbid Age: Britain between the Wars.* London: Penguin Books, 2009.

Piketty, Thomas. *Capital in the Twenty-First Century.* Cambridge, MA: Belknap Press of Harvard University Press, 2014.

Prigozy, Ruth. "Fitzgerald's Flappers and Flapper Films of the Jazz Age: Behind the Morality." In *A Historical Guide to F. Scott Fitzgerald*, edited by Kirk Curnutt. Oxford: Oxford University Press, 2004.

Recent Social Trends in the United States: Report of the President's Research Committee on Social Trends. 2 vols. Westport, CT: Greenwood Press, 1970.

Ring, Frances Kroll. *Against the Current: As I Remember F. Scott Fitzgerald.* Berkeley, CA: Creative Arts Book Company, 1987.

Robinson, Forrest G. *Love's Story Told: A Life of Henry A. Murray.* Cambridge, MA: Harvard University Press, 1992.

Royce, Josiah. *The Philosophy of Josiah Royce.* Edited by John K. Roth. Indianapolis: Hackett Publishing, 1982.

Russell, Bertrand. *The Analysis of Mind.* London: Routledge, 2002.

Ryan, Alan. *John Dewey and the High Tide of American Liberalism.* New York: W. W. Norton, 1995.

Salmose, Niklas. "Reading Nostalgia: Textual Memory in *The Great Gatsby.*" *F. Scott Fitzgerald Review* 12 (2014): 67–87.

Santayana, George. *Character and Opinion in the United States.* Garden City, NY: Doubleday, 1956.

———. *The Essential Santayana.* Edited by Martin A. Coleman. Bloomington: Indiana University Press, 2009.

———. *The Genteel Tradition.* Edited by Douglas L. Wilson. Lincoln: University of Nebraska Press, 1998.

Scott, Nancy J. *Georgia O'Keeffe.* London: Reaktion Books, 2015.

Seigfried, Charlene Haddock. "James: Sympathetic Apprehension of the Point of View of the Other." In *Classical American Pragmatism*, edited by Sandra B. Rosenthal, Carl R. Hausman, and Douglas R. Anderson. Urbana: University of Illinois Press, 1999.

Singley, Carol J. *A Historical Guide to Edith Wharton.* New York: Oxford University Press, 2003.

Snyder, Robert W. *The Voice of the City.* Chicago: Ivan Dee, 1989.

Teachout, Terry. *The Skeptic.* New York: HarperCollins, 2002.

Tocqueville, Alexis de. *Democracy in America.* 2 vols. Edited by Henry Reeve. New York: Alfred A. Knopf, 1945.

Tompkins, Jane. *Sensational Designs: The Cultural Work of American Fiction, 1790–1860.* New York: Oxford University Press, 1985.

Trilling, Lionel. *The Moral Obligation to Be Intelligent.* Edited by Leon Wieseltier. New York: Farrar, Straus, Giroux, 2000.

———. *Speaking of Literature and Society.* New York: Harcourt Brace Jovanovich, 1980.

Troy, William. "Scott Fitzgerald—the Authority of Failure." In *Fitzgerald: The Man and His Work,* edited by Alfred Kazin. New York: Collier, 1951.

Turnbull, Andrew. *Scott Fitzgerald.* New York: Charles Scribner's Sons, 1962.

West, James L. W., III. *The Perfect Hour.* New York: Random House, 2006.

Wharton, Edith. *Edith Wharton: Novellas and Other Writings.* Edited by Cynthia Griffin Wolff. New York: Library of America, 1990.

Whitehead, Alfred North. *Science and the Modern World.* New York: Macmillan, 1967.

Wilson, Edmund. *Edmund Wilson: Literary Essays and Reviews of the 1920s and 30s.* Edited by Lewis M. Dabney. New York: Library of America, 2007.

———. *Edmund Wilson: Literary Essays and Reviews of the 1930s and 40s.* Edited by Lewis M. Dabney. New York: Library of America, 2007.

———. *The Higher Jazz.* Edited by Neale Reinitz. Iowa City: University of Iowa Press, 1998.

———. *I Thought of Daisy.* Baltimore: Penguin Books, 1963.

———. *Letters on Literature and Politics, 1912–1972.* Edited by Elena Wilson. New York: Farrar, Straus and Giroux, 1977.

INDEX